How I Learnt To Speak in ENGLISH?

How I Learnt To Speak in ENGLISH?

Techniques that made her FLUENT

NEETU SUGANDH

Notion Press

Old No. 38, New No. 6
McNichols Road, Chetpet
Chennai - 600 031

First Published by Notion Press 2017
Copyright © Neetu Sugandh 2017
All Rights Reserved.

ISBN 978-1-948230-27-8

CONTENTS

MY STORY

I was rejected in my first job interview because of not being able to communicate fluently in English. After a few months, the same company hired me and later on promoted me as a communication trainer to train their employees on spoken English. This started my career as a *communication trainer*. Without any exaggeration, I became one of the best communication trainers in the industry. My trainees were very thankful for my methods of training because they made them learn how to communicate in English correctly throughout their lives. In addition, they knew what to do if they needed to improve further without my help.

Considering that I faced a challenge with communicating in English earlier, I had an advantage while training people on Communication as I understood the mind set and challenges of people who struggled with speaking fluently. I had faced it. So I knew the learners' challenges. This is what made me an excellent trainer of the language. I was able to break things down to the learners' level of understanding and grasping.

Not just this, I created as well as improved existing communication training for a number of organizations. My colleagues, bosses, and clients showed full trust in my techniques of training on communication. Native speakers of English (for whom English is their first language) used to ask me how I could speak so well even though English was not my first language.

This book contains my journey of learning how to communicate in English fluently. I have shared my methods of learning English, especially spoken English. With these methods,

I was able to master the language in a few months. This book also has my notes and examples that helped me remember the concepts and guidelines easily.

I recommend this book to anyone who is interested in learning English in an easy and independent manner or refreshing their English basics quickly. Remember, you can only understand complex rules and increase your vocabulary when you know the basics. It is hard and stressful to jump to Level 2 without completing Level 1. I have explained concepts in the easiest possible manner and have consciously avoided too much information on each topic. What makes this book fun and effective are the techniques through which you will be learning each concept. If you take responsibility for improving your communication, you will automatically enjoy completing the activities. Through the activities, you will notice a change in the way you communicate in English as each day passes. The time that you will take to start showing improvement depends on your level of English as of today and the dedication you show. If you complete the recommended activities on a daily basis, you could learn in one month to three months. It could be lesser if you already know the language and are struggling only with speaking fluently or only with a few grammar rules.

This book is also very helpful for those who train on spoken English and want to understand their learners in a better way.

My journey began with being rejected. Rejection is not a good feeling. I was very demotivated and felt inferior as if I was not good enough to do anything in life. After a few days of thinking, I went into action mode and figured out what I was lacking. Even after getting a fairly decent percentage in school in my English exams, what made me get rejected?

The answer was that I never made an effort to speak in English. I could write without making too many errors but I could never express myself clearly if I were to speak only in English for more than a few seconds. I did not even have many English speakers at home. So I never felt the need to speak in English.

I am not embarrassed to share that not many people in my family know this language well; however it does not make them any less talented. My family was the biggest support system I had which encouraged me to refresh my spoken English skills rather than getting demotivated after I was rejected.

If you want to communicate in English fluently, the first thing to do is to stop feeling inferior just because you don't know the language. Then, figure out the areas in which you are lacking. For example, in my case, it was lack of effort and practice of speaking in English. Different people face a variety of challenges such as not being exposed to the language at all, not having many people around to understand the language, or not being good at Grammar, Pronunciation, or Fluency. Some people also get bored because there are so many rules in the English language and then, there are so many exceptions to the rules. I faced this challenge too.

I did not know where to begin from. There were many thick books that looked scary and made me think that it would probably take a lifetime to complete those lengthy exercises. And there were way too many concepts explained in a lengthy fashion. I felt that those books were great for people who wanted to master the language or write thesis on it but I was looking for something that I could understand easily and remember for the rest of my life. I even thought of going to a language institute for practising English but the length of their training did not get me interested. I did not want to learn English to clear written exams. I wanted to learn how to speak in English fluently.

What caught my eye was a child's English Grammar book. I started making my own notes and writing simple and limited things that I could remember. But there is a lot that I did differently than how I learnt in school. Grammar is vast and there is Pronunciation too. Therefore, I balanced it by learning minimal definitions and focussing on the correct usage. I also completed exercises verbally rather than writing everything down. Then, I started applying what I learnt by talking to people in English as much as I could.

This book is a compilation of the basic concepts of the language and effective tips on improving your English throughout life. It has the flow and methods I followed and the limited, yet effective content I used for learning. This book also has activities that focus on helping you grasp concepts in a better way. Most important, it has common errors that people make on a daily basis. When you review them, it will be easier for you to correct them.

My objective is to help you learn quickly and make you more independent in learning the language. If you follow this book the way it is written, I am sure you will have your story of learning how to speak in English very soon.

An Incident That Inspired Me to Write This Book

After training and writing for about six years, I took a break from my profession to learn makeup. Once I completed my makeup training, I started to work on fashion photoshoots as a makeup artist. There was a young boy who used to observe the shoots. He was in the learning phase of photography. He never used to talk to me much. But he was very comfortable talking to everyone else. It took me some time to figure out that he was shy to say anything to me in the fear that I would say something in English and he wouldn't know how to respond.

Therefore, one day I decided to communicate with him in his first language, Hindi. I was amazed to see how much conversation he made with me. He spoke about his family, how much he enjoyed photography and his girlfriend. Then, he shared something in a very shy manner.

He said, "I fear talking to people who speak in English. I fear that they would make fun of me."

He wanted to learn but could not dedicate much time to learning English. This incident made me get back to training on communication and I decided to write this book. I could see a part of the younger me in that boy. Then I thought of the many people who have so much potential but are not progressing because they are not able to communicate in English effectively.

Don't just learn English from this book. Create your own story of learning this language!

Chapter 1

• • • • • • • • • •

HOW WILL I LEARN?

I say don't worry about how you will you learn, enjoy the learning process.

Remember this statement, "Don't just speak in English; communicate in English. And, you can only do it by thinking in English."

The definition of Communication says, "it's a two way process."

This means that if you are talking to someone in English, the other person should be able to understand you and respond. If they don't, you are only talking; you are not communicating.

One of the main reasons why we speak in English incorrectly is because we don't think in English. When we think in our mother tongue and try to translate it into English, we are only replacing words without really understanding how their order should be. So from now, start thinking in English.

I understand that it's not easy to start thinking in a different language all of a sudden. However, even the word impossible says, "I am possible." Therefore, begin to think in English as much as you can. If you don't know the language at all and find this challenging, you could start as soon as you begin to learn and understand the language a little.

Now the question arises, "Where do I begin from or how will I learn?"

To answer this, I have listed four major areas of the language that are important to speak fluently. Circle the ones you face issues with. It could be one, two, three, or all of them. Don't worry because we will cover all.

- **Grammar**
- **Pronunciation**
- **Fluency**
- **Comprehension**

Without complicating it too much, let me show you the topics that you will be learning under each of them. *Put a tick mark on the topics in the table below each time you complete a chapter.*

When I started learning English, there were so many topics and areas to be learnt that I was confused about where to begin from and how to progress. This table will make the learning more organised.

Some people ask if English can be learnt without learning Grammar. My personal experience says "no." One needs to know Grammar rules to speak grammatically correct English.

Grammar	Pronunciation	Fluency	Comprehension
Nouns	Consonant Sounds	Tips	Tips
Pronouns		Self-Practice	Self-Practice
Verbs	Vowel Sounds		
Subject Verb Agreement	Syllables		
Question Formation	Sentence Stress & Intonation		
	Tone		
	Self-Practice		

Grammar	Pronunciation	Fluency	Comprehension
Adjectives			
Adverbs			
Prepositions			
Articles			
Conjunctions			
Interjections			
Conditionals			

Treat this table like a video game. You complete each level as you complete each chapter.

For those who don't enjoy playing video games, treat this table like your wish list. You will get an item as you complete a chapter.

You have no idea how much you will enjoy ticking these topics as you learn and how happy you will be the day you have a tick on all of them. I was jumping with joy when I completed all of these topics.

Guidelines

- Think in English.
- Follow the book flow. Do not jump to Chapter 2 if you haven't read Chapter 1.
- Complete the recommended exercises; else the learning will not be as effective.
- Focus on recognising the sounds we produce whenever we discuss pronunciation (not the letters from A to Z). I will explain this more when we begin pronunciation.

- Notice that the topics listed under each section in the video game table or the wish list table are actually the parts that make them.
    - Grammar is made up of eight parts of speech written in the table – Nouns, Pronouns, Verbs, Adjectives, Adverbs, Prepositions, Conjunctions and Interjections. The rest of the topics are also important to discuss.
    - Pronunciation is made up of sounds, syllables, sentence stress, intonation, and tone.
    - Fluency and Comprehension tips and exercises are given too.

Hope you enjoy the learning experience!

Chapter 2

• • • • • • • • • •

NOUNS AND CONSONANT SOUNDS

Think of your favourite person. I can guess who that person is if I look at them from a Grammar perspective. That person is a *noun*.

In this section, you will be learning nouns.

Your favourite person could be your wife, husband, daughter, son, friend, mother, father, or someone unknown.

Write who the person is. _______________________________

They are all **common nouns**.

Write the person's name here. _______________________________

The name of your favourite person is a **proper noun**.

Just like your favourite person, things or places that you like are all *common nouns*. But their names are *proper nouns*.

For example, I like *movies* and *home*. These are *common nouns*. Their names such as *Harry Potter* and *India* are *proper nouns*.

Write your favourite things and places. (Common nouns)

____

Write the names of your favourite things and places. (Proper nouns) _______________________________

Notes for Reference

Review the notes below to see examples.

Types of Nouns

Proper nouns refer to the individual name of a person, place or thing.

Common nouns refer to the rest.

Proper Nouns	Common Nouns
Ansh, Ruby, Sheru, India, Harry Potter, 3 Idiots, Sunday.	boy, girl, elephant, dog, country, book, education, birthday.

If you think of common nouns, there are so many of them.

- Things, places, or people that you like or dislike.
- Things that you use.
- Things that you eat.

Even your feelings and state of mind are nouns, for example, *love, hate, happiness, pain, fear.*

There are so many types of common nouns; therefore it's a good idea to recognise how they are divided further.

Learning Tips

- Don't focus on learning definitions.
- Focus on recognising each type of noun through the definitions given.

Common nouns can be divided into: abstract, collective, compound, countable and uncountable nouns.

Countable	Things you can perceive with your five senses and can be counted.

Uncountable	Things that cannot be counted.
Collective	A group of people or things.
Compound	Made up of two or more words.
Abstract	Things you cannot experience with your five senses.

Examples:

Countable
photograph, book, key, phone, case, base

Uncountable
butter, cheese, honey, water, wood, rice

Collective
army, group, band, team, village, school, bunch

Compound
keyboard, mother-in-law, makeup

Abstract
Feeling: love, hate, anger, peace
State: pain, happiness, loyalty, compassion
Events: education, reality
Ideas: truth, faith, belief

Interesting Facts about Abstract Nouns

Friend is a countable noun; however, *friendship* is an abstract noun.

Nouns ending with the following suffixes are often abstract. One example is given for each. Write one more that comes to your mind.

- -tion: **pronunciation**
- -acy: **democracy**
- -ity: **publicity**
- -ship: **ownership**
- -ism: **professionalism**
- -age: **marriage**
- -ment: **agreement**
- -ence: **patience**
- -ance: **tolerance**
- -ness: **sadness**

Activity

1. Look at the things around you and write two examples for each type of noun.
   - Proper nouns:
   - Common nouns:
   - Countable:
   - Uncountable:
   - Collective:
   - Compound:
   - Abstract:

Now that you recognise the different types of nouns, think of what you would say if there was more than one person, place, or thing.

For example, *toy* is a noun; what would you say if there was more than one *toy*?

Please write here. __________

Answer: toys

Beach is a noun; what would you say if there was more than one *beach*?

Please write here. __________

Answer: beaches

Lady is a noun; what would you say if there was more than one *lady*?

Please write here. __________

Answer: ladies

Notes for Reference

Forms of Nouns

Singular form of noun is used when you refer to a single person, place, thing, event, or idea.

Plural form of noun is used when you refer to more than one person, place, thing, event, or idea.

Regular nouns change into plural by:

- Adding **s**

  Examples: boy-boys, book-books

- Adding **es**

  Examples: peach-peaches, tomato- tomatoes

- Adding **ies**

  Examples: lady-ladies, butterfly-butterflies

Irregular nouns change into plural in different ways:

- Man-men
- Wife-wives
- Tooth-teeth
- Person-people
- Cactus-cacti
- Sheep-sheep

- Deer-deer
- Air-air
- Makeup-makeup

The reason for learning singular and plural is to ensure that you don't use it incorrectly in sentences. I have heard many people using noun forms incorrectly.

For example, uncountable nouns cannot be counted and will always be used in singular form. You cannot change *rice* to *rices*.

Let us use it in a few sentences.

- Please give me some *rice*. (Right)
  Please give me some *rices*. (Wrong)

- Your *hair* is very nice. (Right)
  Your *hairs* are very nice. (Wrong)

Similarly, some abstract nouns cannot be used in plural form. You cannot change *education* to *educations*.

- English *education* is important. (Right)
  English *educations* are important. (Wrong)

Now, review some of the common errors made and find out why they are wrong.

Common Errors

- I have *many informations* for you.
- You made me go through a lot of *pains*.
- Sarah gave me many *advices*.
- I saw many *sheeps* crossing the road.
- He is my *cousin brother*.
- Please include your *sign* here.

Wrong	Right	Reason
I have *many informations* for you.	I have *a lot of information* for you.	You cannot count information; therefore, it will remain singular.
You made me go through a lot of *pains*.	You made me go through a lot of *pain*.	You cannot count pain; therefore, it will remain singular.
Sarah gave me many *advices*.	Sarah gave me *some advice*.	You cannot count advice; therefore, it will remain singular.
I saw many *sheeps* crossing the road.	I saw many *sheep* crossing the road.	The plural form of nouns such as sheep, fish, and deer remains the same as their singular form.
He is my *cousin brother*.	He is my *cousin*.	The word *he* tells you that the cousin is a boy. Unnecessary words are not needed.
Please include your *sign* here.	Please include your *signature* here.	Sign and signature are different words. Please don't use *sign* for *signature*.

Listening Activity

One of the reasons why we speak incorrectly is when we hear incorrect English. Therefore, you need to develop a habit of recognising errors as you hear them and correcting them instantly. This activity will help you get started.

1. Read the following sentences loudly. They are wrong.
2. Correct each sentence verbally and check if you are right.

Wrong
I have to set several alarms clocks to wake up.
John is afraid of mouses.
Bobby has two foots.
I don't like persons who don't respect elders.
I have two sister-in-laws.
There are many beautiful womans in town.

Right
I have to set several *alarm clocks* to wake up.
John is afraid of *mice*.
Bobby has two *feet*.
I don't like *people* who don't respect elders.
I have two *sisters-in-law*.
There are many beautiful *women* in town.

Now that you know the common errors associated with nouns, let's find out where we should place the noun while forming sentences. If you noticed, we used nouns mostly at the beginning and end of sentences in the examples given above.

What Is a Sentence Made Up of?

Sentence = Subject + Verb + Object

For example, Ram reads books. (*Ram* is the subject, *reads* is the verb and *books* is the object.)

Notice, the different topics that you will be learning in Grammar are actually parts that make up a sentence. That's why it's important to understand them.

Take a look at the table below.

Subject	Verb	Object
Who performs the action?	What is the action?	Who receives the action?
Ram (noun)	Reads	Books (noun)

Interesting Facts

Sometimes the same word can be used as a noun and verb.

- If it is used as a verb, it means action.
- If it is used as a noun, it means the name of an activity.

For example, in Ram reads books, *reads* is an action. Therefore, it is a verb.

If we say, Ram likes reading, *reading* is the name of an activity. Therefore, it is a noun.

Let's review a few more examples.

- He plays games. (*Play* is a verb, *games* is a noun.)
  He enjoys playing. (*Playing* is a noun.)

- She selects fruits. (*Select* is a verb, *fruits* is a noun.)
  Fruit selection is her job. (*Fruit selection* is a noun; *job* is a noun.)

Learning Tips

- In Grammar, the same word can be a noun or verb depending on how we are using it.
- Remember these simple rules.
  - If a word is showing an action, it is a verb.
  - If a word is naming an activity, it is a noun.

Activity:

Keeping the Subject + Verb + Object rule in mind, form one simple sentence with the following nouns. An example is given.

Job: I love my *job*.

Child: That *child* is very talented.

Education: Basic *education* is needed to do anything in life.

Email: Your *email* was rude.

People: The *people* in this house are very caring.

English: I can speak in *English*.

Paper: I need a blank sheet of *paper*.

Learning Tips

- Think and speak in English as much as you can.
- There are many nouns. It's not possible to cram each of them along with their plural forms. You will learn more with time as you begin to communicate in English.
- Whenever you find a noun for which you do not know the plural form, make a note of it here. Find out its plural using an online dictionary. You can also listen to how the word is pronounced.

Personal Notes

____

____

____

____

Pronunciation Time

If you want to effectively communicate in English, grammar should go hand in hand with pronunciation. In addition, it's very boring to learn only grammar without knowing how the words are pronounced. Therefore, you will be applying concepts you learn in grammar in the pronunciation section.

I mentioned earlier to follow the flow of the book. It will help you learn faster and make you confident in your overall English.

Letters Versus Sounds

The letters in the English alphabet are given below.

A	B	C	D	E	F	G	H	I	J
K	L	M	N	O	P	Q	R	S	T
U	V	W	X	Y					

How many are letters are there?______

How many of them are consonants?_____

How many are vowels?______

There are 26 letters in the English alphabet out of which A, E, I, O, U are vowels. This means there are 5 vowels and 21 consonants.

Interesting Fact

- These 26 letters produce around 40 sounds (16 vowel sounds and 24 consonant sounds). Different accents many have different number of sounds. Don't get confused with the number. Simply focus on pronouncing the sounds given correctly.

Let's take an example of a noun to learn the difference between letters and sounds.

Note: The letters are written in capitals and the sounds are written in small case so that you can differentiate.

Say *mat* loudly. What you are producing are sounds, not letters.

In the word, *mat*:

- The letters are: M, A, T.
- The sounds are: m(ae)t. (The sound of *m* and *t* are consonant sounds. There is a vowel sound given here too. We will discuss it in the next chapter.)

Similarly, in the word, *cat*:

- The letters are: C, A, T.
- The sounds are: k(ae)t.
- The consonant *C* is producing the sound *k* and the consonant *T* is producing the sound *t*.

Let us begin pronunciation with the 24 consonant sounds.

How Are Sounds Produced?

We use our mouth, tongue, and teeth to produce sounds.

How Is Each Sound Different?

The way we use our mouth, tongue, and teeth determines the sound we produce. When we use them in different ways, we can produce different sounds.

Take a look at the chart below.

- Consonant sounds can be voiced and unvoiced.
- **Voiced sounds** occur when the vocal cords vibrate while the sound is being produced.
- There is no vocal cord vibration when producing **unvoiced sounds**.

Notice that most sounds in the chart are given in pairs: p and b, k and g, t and d, f and v, s and z, th and th(e), sh and zh, ch and j. That's because these sounds are produced in exactly the same manner. The only difference is that one is unvoiced and the other is voiced. Therefore, it is important to test if your pronunciation is different when you pronounce these sounds. Else, they will sound the same.

Test 1: Place your hand on your throat as you say the words. When saying the voiced sounds, you should be able to feel a vibration on your throat. When saying the unvoiced sounds you sound not be able to feel a vibration.

Test 2: Put your hand in front of your mouth. You will feel a gush of air on your hand while saying the unvoiced sounds. You will not feel a gush of air while saying the voiced sounds.

Consonant Sounds Chart with Nouns as Examples

Unvoiced	Voiced
p (pen)	**b** (bet)
k (kite)	**g** (gate)
t (time)	**d** (date)
f (fox)	**v** (voucher)
s (strand)	**z** (zebra)
th (theory)	**th**(e) (father)
sh (shoe)	**zh** (treasure)
ch (chicken)	**j** (jet)
h (hen)	**l** (lane)
	m (mat)
	n (nose)
	ng (ring)
	r (car)
	w (water)
	y (Yugoslavia)

Activity

1. Open an online dictionary on your computer.
2. Listen to the pronunciation of each word in the chart. Try to recognise the sound when you do this.

3. Practise pronouncing the word till you master its pronunciation.

4. Go horizontally so that you can differentiate between voiced and unvoiced sounds.

My Experience: When I learnt sounds, the different phonetic symbols confused me. Therefore, I suggest that you learn using the Consonant Sounds chart given in this book. If you are confused, you can refer to the words given as examples in the chart.

Activity

1. Once you have mastered the words in the chart, write one new word that has the sound at the beginning, one word that has the sound in the middle, and one word that has the sound at the end. Examples are given for your reference.

2. Listen to the pronunciation of the words you write using an online dictionary.

3. Practise pronouncing the words till you master their pronunciation.

p (Unvoiced)	b (Voiced)
pet, spike, keep	but, noble, rob

k (Unvoiced)	g (Voiced)
kiss, school, shock	girl, giggle, leg

t (Unvoiced)	d (Voiced)
time, strike, test	day, riddle, rod

f (Unvoiced)	v (Voiced)
fake, suffer, roof	vain, river, love

s (Unvoiced)	z (Voiced)
smart, rest, press	zodiac, reason, prize

th (Unvoiced)	th(e) (Voiced)
thank, healthy, earth	that, either, breathe

sh (Unvoiced)	zh (Voiced)
shock, motion, rush	genre, decision, beige

ch (Unvoiced)	j (Voiced)
cheap, kitchen, rich	jelly, magic, marriage

h (Unvoiced)
hike, rehearsal, ah

l (Voiced)
late, belly, tell

m (Voiced)
must, grammar, scam

n (Voiced)
noise, tender, rain

ng (Voiced)
English, reading (Note: Words do not begin with this sound.)

r (Voiced)
write, crazy, car

w (Voiced)
wake, awake (Note: Words do not end with this sound.)

y (Voiced)
yes, royal, (Note: Words do not end with this sound.)

Activity

1. Practise the sounds further by saying the following words loudly in pairs.

2. Stress on the highlighted sounds and pronounce them in a crisp manner.

3. Notice how the meaning changes with the change in sound.

Sounds p and b	Sounds b and v	Sounds d and j
• pit, bit	• bat, vat	• dog, jog
• pay, bay	• berry, very	• dam, jam
• pill, bill	• bet, vet	• dump, jump
• pat, bat	• boat, vote	• paid, page
Sounds j and z	Sounds s and sh	Sounds s and th
• wage, ways	• sign, shine	• sink, think
• forge, fours	• sit, shit	• sank, thank
• page, pays	• see, she	• sick, thick
• fridge, frizz	• so, show	• tense, tenth

Sounds z and th	Sounds f and v	Sounds f and th
• close, clothes • zen, then • bays, bathe • breeze, breathe	• fine, vine • fat, vat • fast, vast • fan, van	• free, three • fought, thought • fin, thin • first, thirst
Sounds t and d • ten, den • mat, mad • got, god • sent, send	**Sounds k and g** • Kate, gate • sink, sing • came, game • coat, goat	**Sounds ch and j** • chain, Jane • choice, Joyce • chest, jest • chill, Jill
Sounds ch and t • chip, tip • chest, test • chill, till • beach, beat	**Sounds l and r** • fly, fry • lane, rain • law, raw • late, rate	**Sounds m and n** • mine, nine • am, an • lime, line • sum, sun
Sounds n and ng • sin, sing • win, wing • pin, ping • thin, thing	**Sounds t and th** • tank, thank • tin, thin • team, theme • taught, thought	**Sounds d and th(e)** • doze, those • den, then • day, they • ladder, lather
Sounds v and w • vow, wow • vent, went • vine, wine • very, worry		
Note: v and w are two different sounds. Many people pronounce them in the same way. Put each word in an online dictionary and recognise the difference.		

Learning Tips

- Say the pairs given above out loud *on a daily basis* till you are very comfortable with consonant sounds.

- Stress on pronouncing the highlighted sounds clearly while ensuring they are crisp. Remember, consonant sounds are short and crisp sounds.

- Make it a habit to pronounce consonant sounds correctly each time you communicate in English.

- Make a note of sounds you face a challenge with. You will be able to master them if you practise.

- Refer to one good online dictionary while learning pronunciation.

Self-Practice Activity

Watch a good English movie to get comfortable with sounds. It will also help you understand the language better. Look at the subtitles if you face a challenge with understanding the movie. If not in the first go, you will start understanding and enjoying English movies the more you watch them.

Now you can go back to the video game or wish list table given in Chapter 1 and tick Nouns and Consonant Sounds.

Chapter 3

. . . .

PRONOUNS AND VOWEL SOUNDS

Take a look at this sentence.

Raj needs to practise so that Raj is able to communicate more effectively with Raj's clients.

Doesn't this sound awkward?

Therefore, we use pronouns. A pronoun is a word that is used in place of a noun.

Raj needs to practice so that *he* is able to communicate more effectively with *his* clients.

Doesn't this sound better?

In this section, you will be learning pronouns.

Take a look at the table below. It has the most commonly used pronouns.

	Subject	Object	Possessive	Reflexive
Singular				
1st Person	I	Me	Mine, My	Myself
2nd person	You	You	Yours, Your	Yourself

	Subject	Object	Possessive	Reflexive
Singular				
3rd person	He, She, It	Him, Her, It	His, Hers, Its	Himself, Herself, Itself
Plural				
1st Person	We	Us	Ours	Ourselves
2nd person	You	You	Yours	Yourselves
3rd person	They	Them	Theirs	Themselves

First, let's find out more about first person, second person, and third person.

Assume you are talking to someone. You will be referred to as the **first person**.

The person with whom you are talking is the **second person**.

If you and the second person are talking about someone else, that person will be the **third person**.

Read the following examples out loud to grasp better.

- *I* won the prize. (The word *I* is the first person.)
- *You* won the second prize. (The word *you* is the second person.)
- *She* won the third prize. (The word *she* is the third person.)

Now, assume that you and your friend are talking as one team to a few other people.

In this case, you and your friend will become the **first person** (in plural form, that is, *we*).

The other people with whom you are talking become the **second person** (in plural form, that is, *you*).

If you and the second person are talking about some other people, those people will be the **third person** (in plural form, that is, *they*).

Read the following examples out loud to grasp better.

- *We* won the prize. (The word *we* is the first person in plural form.)
- *You* won the second prize. (The word *you* is the second person in plural form.)
- *They* won the third prize. (The word *they* is the third person in plural form.)

Just like nouns, pronouns change their form when there is more than one person or thing involved.

- *I* becomes *we*.
- *You* stays as *you*.
- *He, she,* or *it* becomes *they*.

Now let's proceed to the four types of pronouns given in the table.

Do you remember this formula from the previous chapter?

What Is a Sentence Made Up of?

Sentence = Subject + Verb + Object

Similar to nouns, pronouns either act as subjects or objects in a sentence.

When pronouns act as subjects, they are referred to as **subjective pronouns**.

For example:

- *I* sent the email.
- *You* sent the email.
- *He/She/It* sent the email.
- *We* sent the email.
- *They* sent the email.

When pronouns act as objects, they are referred to as **objective pronouns**.

For example:

- Mary taught *me*.
- Mary taught *you*.
- Mary taught *him/her/it*.
- Mary taught *us*.
- Mary taught *them*.

When pronouns show possession, they are referred to as **possessive pronouns**.

For example:

- She returned *my* book because it is *mine*.
- The book is *yours*.

Common Errors and Guidelines

- We do **not** use *me* as a subject. For example:
  - *You* and *me* will go. (Wrong)
    You and *I* will go. (Right)

- We do **not** use *I, he, or she* as objects. For example:
  - *I* like her more than *he*. (Wrong)
    I like her more than *him*. (Right)

  - The conversation stays between *you* and *I*. (Wrong)
    The conversation stays between *you* and *me*. (Right)

- Whenever we use *I* with another subject, *I* always comes in the end. For example:
  - *I* and *Bryan* will dance. (Wrong)
    Bryan and *I* will dance. (Right)

  - *I, Ram,* and *Geeta* will study. (Wrong)
    Ram, Geeta, and *I* will study. (Right)

Interesting Fact

Possessive pronouns are technically adjectives as they modify a noun. You will better understand this when you learn adjectives.

Now let us understand what **reflexive pronouns** are.

What is the meaning of the word *reflection*? It means "throw back." Reflexive pronouns are objects that refer to the subject. I understand them like this: when the subject is doing something to itself.

For example:

- I thanked *myself* for learning English.
- Rashmi praised *herself* for being humble.
- You should copy *yourself* on the email.

Notice that these pronouns are used as objects and are referring to the subjects. They are a necessary part of the sentence.

Common Errors and Guidelines

> myself, yourself, himself, herself, itself, ourselves, yourselves, themselves

- We do **not** use words given above as subjects. For example:
  - *Myself* Sheela. (Wrong)
    I am Sheela. (Right)

  - Rakesh and *myself* will attend the meeting. (Wrong)
    Rakesh and *I* will attend the meeting. (Right)

- We do **not** use words given above when we describe things people usually do for themselves, such as bathe, shave, brush. For example:
  - I bathe *myself* each day. (Wrong)
    I bathe each day. (Right)

- He shaves *himself.* (Wrong)

  He shaves. (Right)

- They brush *themselves.* (Wrong)

  They brush. (Right)

Activity

1. Make one simple sentence with each pronoun given in the Pronouns table.

2. Refer to the notes given above if needed. An example is given for your reference.

I: *I* read a book.

You (as singular, subject): *You* read a book.

He: *He* reads a book.

She: *She* reads a book.

It (as singular, subject): *It* was good.

We: *We* read a book.

You (as plural, subject): *You* read a book.

They: *They* read a book.

Me: Nora scolded *me.*

You (as singular, object): Nora scolded *you.*

Him: Nora scolded *him.*

Her: Nora scolded *her.*

It (as singular, object): Nora gave *it.*

Us: Nora scolded *us.*

You (as plural, object): Nora scolded *you.*

Them: Nora scolded *them.*

Mine: The pen is *mine.*

My: It is *my* pen.

Yours: The pen is *yours.*

Your: It is *your* pen.

His: It is *his* pen.

Hers: The pen is *hers.*

Its: The pen and *its* needle are great.

Ours: The pens are *ours.*

Yours: The pens are *yours.*

Theirs: The pens are *theirs.*

Myself: I gave *myself* unnecessary trouble.

Yourself: You gave *yourself* unnecessary trouble.

Himself: He gave *himself* unnecessary trouble.

Herself: She gave *herself* unnecessary trouble.

Itself: The dog gave *itself* unnecessary trouble.

Ourselves: We gave *ourselves* unnecessary trouble.

Yourselves: You gave *yourselves* unnecessary trouble.

Themselves: They gave *themselves* unnecessary trouble.

There are a few more types of pronouns. We will be reviewing each of them as there are many errors that people make while using pronouns.

- **Intensive Pronouns**
- **Reciprocal Pronouns**
- **Indefinite Pronouns**
- **Interrogative Pronouns**
- **Relative Pronouns**
- **Demonstrative Pronouns**

Learning Tip: Focus on using pronouns correctly. It is completely alright if you are not able to memorise the definitions. What's important is that you understand their correct usage.

You just learnt that reflexive pronouns are used as objects that refer to the subject.

Reflexive pronouns (myself, herself, yourself, and so on) change to **intensive pronouns** when they emphasise another noun or pronoun, for example:

- I learnt from Amitabh Bachchan *himself.*
- I *myself* don't like her.

In the examples above, *himself* and *myself* are putting stress on the noun **Amitabh Bachchan** and on the pronoun, **I**. They are not referring to them.

Interesting Fact: You could remove the intensive pronoun from a sentence, and the sentence would still make sense.

Remember: A word can change its type depending on how it is used in a sentence. Like in case of nouns, we learnt that *friend* is a common noun but *friendship* is an abstract noun. Similarly, words like myself, herself, yourself, and so on are reflexive pronouns if they refer to the subject and they are intensive pronouns if they emphasise another noun or pronoun.

Let's review a few more examples.

Reflexive Pronoun	Intensive Pronoun
She bought *herself* a watch.	She *herself* bought a watch.
Abhishek got *himself* a dog.	Abhishek *himself* got a dog.
I taught *myself* some English.	I *myself* taught some English.
Make a sentence:	Make a sentence:
Make a sentence:	Make a sentence:

A word of caution: Sometimes people use intensive pronouns in a sentence even when they are not required. Read the conversation below.

A: Where are you from?

B: I am from Delhi *itself.* (Wrong)

C: I am from Delhi. (Right)

B is grammatically incorrect because there is no need to put stress on Delhi unnecessarily.

Let us review **reciprocal pronouns.**

What is the meaning of the word *reciprocate*? It means "give or do in return." We use reciprocal pronouns when each of two or more subjects is acting in the same way towards the other. For example, Abhishek is helping Radha, and Radha is helping Abhishek. And we say:

- Abhishek and Radha are helping *each other.*
- Abhishek and Radha are helping *one another.*

There are two reciprocal pronouns. They are both two words.

- Each other
- One another

Interesting Fact: Traditionally, we used *each other* when referring to two people and *one another* when referring more than two people, but this distinction is disappearing in modern English. Now, it's considered alright to use them in place of each other.

Activity: Make a sentence with each of the reciprocal pronouns to grasp better.

Each other: _______________________________________

One another:_______________________________________

Let us review **indefinite pronouns.**

What is the meaning of the word *indefinite*? It means "not clearly defined." Indefinite pronouns are words which replace nouns without specifying which noun they replace. For example:

- *Someone* called me. (*Someone* is an indefinite pronoun as we do not know who called.)
- *One* of the boys clapped. (*One* is an indefinite pronoun as we do not know who clapped.)

Look at the words in the table below. All of them are indefinite pronouns.

> somebody, someone, something, another, anybody, anyone, anything, each, either, neither, everybody, everyone, everything, little, much, no one, nobody, nothing, one, other, others, both, few, many, several, none, most, more, any, all, some

Just like other pronouns, indefinite pronouns can be singular or plural.

Singular	Plural	Singular or Plural
somebody, someone, something, another, anybody, anyone, anything, each, either, neither, everybody, everyone, everything, little, much, no one, nobody, nothing, one, other	others, both, few, many, several	none, most, more, any, all, some
Examples		
Neither of the girls is polite.	*Many* of the girls are polite.	*All* of the people are good.
One of the boys cleaned his hands.	*Few* of the boys cleaned their hands.	*All* of the population is good.

- We always say, one of the *girls* or one of the *boys*. We do not say one of the *girl* or one of the *boy*. The nouns are in their plural form because we are referring to one amongst many.

Neither of the **girls** is polite.	*Many* of the **girls** are polite.
One of the **boys** cleaned his hands.	*Few* of the **boys** cleaned their hands.

- When the pronoun is used as a *singular subject*, we use a *singular verb* or *singular pronoun*.

Right	Wrong	Explanation
Neither of the girls **is** polite.	*Neither* of the girls **are** polite.	*Neither* is a singular pronoun, so we will use a singular verb, *is*.
All of the population **is** good.	*All* of the population **are** good.	In this case, *all* is a singular pronoun, so we will use a singular verb, *is*.
One of the boys cleaned **his** hands.	*One* of the boys cleaned **their** hands.	*One* is a singular pronoun, so we will use a singular pronoun, *his*.

- When the pronoun is used as a *plural subject*, we use a *plural verb or plural pronoun*.

Right	Wrong	Explanation
Many of the girls **are** polite.	*Many* of the girls **is** polite.	*Many* is a plural pronoun, so we will use a plural verb, *are*.
All of the people **are** good.	*All* of the people **is** good.	In this case, *all* is a plural pronoun, so we will use a plural verb, *are*.

Right	Wrong	Explanation
Few of the boys cleaned **their** hands.	*Few* of the boys cleaned **his** hands.	*Few* is a plural pronoun, so we will use a plural pronoun, *their*.

Listening Activity

Remember, you must develop a habit of recognising errors as you hear them and correcting them instantly. This activity will help you practise.

1. Read the following sentences loudly. They are wrong.

2. Correct each sentence verbally and check if you are right.

Wrong
One of the girl made fun of me.
Both the boy speak English.
Everyone are alright.
Most of the butter are stale.
One of the girls gave me their book.
Both of them is shocked.
Many of the boy is taking part in the competition.
Few of the girls gave me her book.

Right
One of the *girls* made fun of me.
Both the *boys* speak English.
Everyone *is* alright.
Most of the butter *is* stale.
One of the girls gave me *her* book.
Both of them *are* shocked.
Many of the *boys are* taking part in the competition.
Few of the girls gave me *their* books.

Activity: Make a sentence with the following pronouns to grasp better.

Anyone: ____

Many: ____

Most: ____

All: ____

Some: ____

Let us review **interrogative pronouns.**

The term *interrogate* means "to ask someone questions to get personal or secret information from them." As the name suggests, we use **interrogative** pronouns to ask questions.

who, whom, whose, which, what

Examples:

- *Who* do you think is the best?
- *Whom* should I contact?
- *Which* book did you read?
- *What* is your name?
- *Whose* book is this?

Common Errors

A very common confusion is whether to use who or whom, for example:

Who **did you see?**	*or*	*Whom* **did you see?**

The right one is: **Whom did you see?**

Here is how to understand it easily. Remember, who = he and whom = him.

- If the answer to your question is *he*, then use *who*.
- If the answer to your question is *him*, then use *whom*.

Let's review the questions again.

Wrong	Right
Who did you see? I saw *he*. (Wrong)	*Whom* did you see? I saw *him*. (Right)
Who will you select? I will select *he*. (Wrong)	*Whom* will you select? I will select *him*. (Right)
Whom will take part? *Him* will take part. (Wrong)	*Who* will take part? *He* will take part. (Right)
Whom will go there? *Him* will go there. (Wrong)	*Who* will go there? *He* will go there. (Right)

Activity: Create questions with the following pronouns to grasp better.

Who:

Whom:

Whose:

Which:

What:

Listening Activity

Remember, you must develop a habit of recognising errors as you hear them and correcting them instantly. This activity will help you practise.

1. Read the following questions loudly. They are wrong.

2. Recall the "who = he and whom = him" rule.

3. Correct each question verbally and check if you are right.

Wrong
Whom is your friend?
Who will they call?

Wrong
Whom is your favourite person?
Who should the teacher trust?

Right
Who is your friend? (*He* is my friend.)
Whom will they call? (They will call *him/them*.)
Who is your favourite person? (*He* is my favourite person.)
Whom should the teacher trust? (The teacher should trust *him*.)

Let us review **relative pronouns**.

As the name suggest, relative pronouns relate to a noun.

who, whom, whose, which, that, whoever, whomever

Examples:

- The lesson *that* I studied today was very helpful.
- The boy *who* met us yesterday was polite.
- The boy *whom* we met yesterday was polite.
- Dance with *whoever* gives you his hand.
- Dance with *whomever* you like.

Common Errors

A very common confusion is between the use of who or whom and whoever or whomever.

Follow the same rule of who/whoever = he and whom/whomever = him to clear your confusion.

- If the answer to your question is *he*, then use *who* or *whoever*.
- If the answer to your question is *him*, then use *whom* or *whomever*.

Let's understand this better through the examples above.

The boy *who* met us yesterday was polite.	Who met us? *He.* Therefore, we have used *who.*
The boy *whom* we met yesterday was polite.	Whom did we meet? *Him.* Therefore, we have used *whom.*
Dance with *whoever* gives you his hand.	Who will give you his hand? *He.* Therefore, we have used *whoever.*
Dance with *whomever* you like.	Whom will you like? *Him.* Therefore, we have used *whomever.*

Interesting Fact: Words such as *who* and *whom* change from interrogative to relative pronouns when used in a sentence.

Activity: Create sentences with the following pronouns to grasp better.

Who:

Whom:

Whoever:

Whomever:

Listening Activity

Remember, you must develop a habit of recognising errors as you hear them and correcting them instantly. This activity will help you practise.

1. Read the following sentences loudly. They are wrong.
2. Recall the "who/whoever = he and whom/whomever = him" rule.
3. Correct each sentence verbally and check if you are right.

Wrong
The girl whom spoke in class was beautiful.
The girl who you like is beautiful.

Wrong
Send the email to whomever is the best.
Send the email to whoever you consider the best.

Right
The girl *who* spoke in class was beautiful. (*She* spoke in class. Therefore, we have used *who*.)
The girl *whom* you like is beautiful. (You like *her*. Therefore, we have used *whom*.)
Send the email to *whoever* is the best. (*He/she* is the best. Therefore, we have used *whoever*.)
Send the email to *whomever* you consider the best. (You consider *him/her* the best. Therefore, we have used *whomever*.)

Let us review **demonstrative pronouns**.

Demonstrative pronouns point towards a noun phrase.

This(Singular)	**That**(Singular)
These(Plural)	**Those**(Plural)

Examples:

- The dress you are wearing is nice. > *This* is nice.
- The boy's bag is green. > *That* is green.
- The flowers on my dress mean a lot to me. > *These* mean a lot to me.
- The days on which we ate pasta were amazing. > *Those* were amazing.

Remember: *This* and *these* are used when we are talking about things close to us in terms of distance or time. When things are far, we use *that* and *those*.

Interesting Fact: Note how demonstrative pronouns completely replace a noun phrase. However, if they are followed by a noun, they will change from demonstrative pronouns to demonstrative adjectives. This is because they would modify a noun in that case. Look at the table below to see examples.

Demonstrative Pronouns	Demonstrative Adjectives
This is nice.	*This* dress is nice.
That is green.	*That* bag is green.
These mean a lot to me.	*These* flowers mean a lot to me.
Those were amazing.	*Those* days were amazing.

Activity: Create sentences with the following pronouns to grasp better.

This:

That:

These:

Those:

Listening Activity

1. Read the following sentences loudly.

2. Replace the noun phrases (in bold) with *this, that, these, those*.

3. Check to see if you are right.

The drawing you made is gorgeous.
The oranges Ruby brings are the best.
The circles you have made are not even.
The map on the table is dirty.

Answers
This is gorgeous.
Those are the best.
These are not even.
That is dirty.

Listening Activity

In this chapter, we have covered a variety of errors made while using pronouns. Given below is a list of the errors we discussed along with what is right.

1. Read the wrong sentence or question loudly without looking at the correct one.

2. Correct it verbally and check to see if you are right.

3. Repeat the process for all the sentences or questions.

4. Refer to the notes in the chapter if you get stuck.

Wrong	Right
The book is your.	The book is *yours*.
You and me will go.	*You* and *I* will go.
I like her more than he.	*I* like her more than *him*.
The conversation stays between you and I.	The conversation stays between *you* and *me*.
I and Bryan will dance.	*Bryan* and *I* will dance.
I, Ram and Geeta will study.	*Ram, Geeta,* and *I* will study.
Myself Sheela.	*I* am Sheela.
Rakesh and myself will attend the meeting.	Rakesh and *I* will attend the meeting.
I bathe myself each day.	*I* bathe each day.
He shaves himself.	*He* shaves.
They brush themselves.	*They* brush.
I am from Delhi itself.	*I* am from Delhi.
Neither of the girl is polite.	Neither of the *girls is* polite.
Neither of the girls are polite.	Neither of the girls *is* polite.
All of the population are good.	*All* of the population *is* good.
One of the boys cleaned their hands.	*One* of the boys cleaned *his* hands.
Many of the girls is polite.	Many of the girls *are* polite.

Wrong	Right
All of the people is good.	All of the people *are* good.
Few of the boys cleaned his hands.	Few of the boys cleaned *their* hands.
One of the girl made fun of me.	One of the *girls* made fun of me.
Both the boy speak English.	Both the *boys* speak English.
Everyone are alright.	Everyone *is* alright.
Most of the butter are stale.	Most of the butter *is* stale.
One of the girls gave me their book.	One of the girls gave me *her* book.
Both of them is shocked.	Both of them *are* shocked.
Many of the boy is taking part in the competition.	Many of the *boys are* taking part in the competition.
Few of the girls gave me her book.	Few of the girls gave me *their* books.
Who did you see?	*Whom* did you see?
Who will you select?	*Whom* will you select?
Whom will take part?	*Who* will take part?
Whom will go there?	*Who* will go there?
Whom is your friend?	*Who* is your friend?
Who will they call?	*Whom* will they call?
Whom is your favourite person?	*Who* is your favourite person?
Who should the teacher trust?	*Whom* should the teacher trust?
The girl whom spoke in class was beautiful.	The girl *who* spoke in class was beautiful.
The girl who you like is beautiful.	The girl *whom* you like is beautiful.

Wrong	Right
Send the email to whomever is the best.	Send the email to *whoever* is the best.
Send the email to whoever you consider the best.	Send the email to *whomever* you consider the best.

Learning Tips

- Think and speak in English as much as you can.
- Review the common errors made while using pronouns at least once a week.
- Do not speak incorrectly if you hear others speak incorrectly. Get into the habit of identifying errors.
- Whenever you get confused while using pronouns, review the notes again.
- Make a note of anything new that you discover related to pronouns in the section below.

Personal Notes

____

____

____

____

Pronunciation Time

As I mentioned earlier, grammar should go hand in hand with pronunciation to communicate in English effectively. Let's apply the concepts of grammar in the pronunciation section.

Before we learn a new topic, recall the following:

- How many letters are there in the English alphabet? **26**
- How many of them are consonants? **21**
- How many are vowels? **5**

- Which are the vowels? **A, E, I, O, U**
- How many vowel sounds do these five vowels produce? **16**

Note: Different accents many have different number of sounds. Don't get confused with the number. Simply focus on pronouncing the sounds given correctly.

We will be covering sixteen vowel sounds in the Pronunciation section.

Learning Tips: Before we begin vowel sounds, I recommend that you practise the consonant sounds by using the charts and examples given in the previous chapter.

Do you remember the difference between letters and sounds?

Let's take an example of a pronoun to differentiate.

Note: The letters are written in capitals and the sounds are written in small case so that you can differentiate.

Say the word *it* loudly. What you are producing are sounds, not letters.

In the word, *it*:

- The letters are: I, T.
- The sounds are: (ih)t. The word has the vowel sound *(ih)* with the consonant sound, *t*.

In the last chapter, we learnt that consonant sounds can be voiced and unvoiced.

Take a look at the chart below.

- All vowel sounds are voiced. This means the vocal cords vibrate when they are produced.
- Vowel sounds can be short or long, for example the sound in the word *they*, is a long vowel sound and the sound in the word *that*, is a short vowel sound.

- Under short vowel sounds, take a look at the schwa sound in the word, *us*. The *uh* sound or the schwa sound is one of the shortest sounds. However, when it is followed by the letter *R*, it neither remains long nor short. It becomes *er*. You will find the *er* sound in the word, *her*.

- Take a look at diphthongs. A diphthong is a sound made by combining two vowel sounds. It comes from the Greek word diphthongs which means "having two sounds." In simple words, it is a combination of two vowel sounds.

Learning Tips

- Whenever you pronounce long vowel sounds, elongate them and open your mouth as much as you can.

- Whenever you pronounce short vowel sounds, keep them crisp as they are short sounds.

- Whenever you pronounce consonant sounds, keep them crisp too as they are crisp sounds.

- Don't focus on the spelling; focus on the sound, for example, the word *who* has only one *O* but it has the long vowel sound *oo*.

Vowel Sounds Chart with Pronouns and Nouns as Examples

Long	Short
ay (**they**)	ae (**that**)
ee (**she**)	eh (**them**)
ai (**mine**)	ih (**it**)
oh (**both**)	aw (**all**)
oo (**you**)	o (**book**) – Book is a noun.
ew (**few**)	uh (**us**)– schwa
aa (**car**) – Car is a noun.	
Schwa followed by the letter R	

er (her)
Diphthongs
oy (b**oy**) – Boy is a noun. (Made by combining aw and ay.)
ow (c**ow**) – Cow is a noun. (Made by combining aa and oh.)

Activity

1. Open an online dictionary on your computer.

2. Listen to the pronunciation of each word in the table. Try to recognise the sound when you do this.

3. Practise pronouncing the word till you master its pronunciation.

4. Go horizontally so that you can differentiate between long and short sounds.

My Experience: When I learnt sounds, the different phonetic symbols confused me. Therefore, I suggest that you learn using the Vowel Sound chart given in this book. If you are confused, you can always refer to the words given as examples in the chart.

Activity

1. Once you have mastered the words in the chart, write two new words that have the vowel sound. Examples are given for your reference.

2. Listen to the pronunciation of the words you write using an online dictionary.

3. Practise pronouncing the words till you master their pronunciation.

ay (Long)
may, way

ee (Long)
he, we

ai (Long)
line, wine

oh (Long)
go, row

oo (Long)
cool, flute

ew (Long)
cute, mute

aa (Long)
vast, task

ae (Short)
bat, mat

eh (Short)
bet, pet

ih (Short)
bit, pit

aw (Short)
ball, boss

o (Short)
would, put

uh (Short)
one, much

er (Neither Long nor Short)
bird, curd

oy (Diphthong)
foil, joy

ow (Diphthong)
how, now

Activity

1. Practise the sounds further by saying the following words loudly in pairs.

2. Elongate the long vowel sounds while keeping the short vowel sounds and consonant sounds crisp.

3. Notice how the meaning changes with the change in sound.

Sounds ih and ee	Sounds eh and ay	Sounds eh and ih
• bit, beat	• bell, bail	• bet, bit
• fit, feet	• wet, wait	• left, lift
• hit, heat	• sell, sale	• tell, till
• it, eat	• pen, pain	• fell, fill
Sounds aw and oh	**Sounds ae and uh**	**Sounds ae and eh**
• not, no	• cat, cut	• man, men
• saw, so	• match, much	• sad, said
• raw, row	• hat, hut	• bad, bed
• for, four	• ran, run	• had, head
Sounds aa and er		
• heart, hurt		
• park, perk		
• cart, curt		
• fast, first		

Learning Tips

- Say the pairs given above out loud *on a daily basis* till you are very comfortable with vowel sounds. However, don't forget to practise the consonant sounds.

- Elongate the long vowel sounds while keeping the short vowel sounds and consonant sounds crisp.

- Make it a habit to pronounce consonant and vowel sounds correctly each time you communicate in English.

- Make a note of sounds you face a challenge with. You will be able to master them if you practise.

- Refer to one good online dictionary while learning pronunciation.

Self-Practice Activity

Watch another good English movie to get comfortable with sounds. It will also help you understand the language better.

Now you can go back to the video game or wish list table given in Chapter 1 and tick Pronouns and Vowel Sounds.

Chapter 4

• • • • • • • • • •

VERBS AND SYLLABLES

You learnt that your favourite person is a noun (child, mother, or friend) and words that you use in place of them are pronouns (he, she, her, or it).

Now think about the things that you would want to do for your favourite person. Cook? Study? Smile? Jump? All of these actions are verbs. Verbs are also called doing words because they show some sort of action.

Do you remember this formula from the previous chapter?

What Is a Sentence Made Up of?

Sentence = Subject + Verb + Object

Therefore, verb forms a crucial part of sentence construction. Think about it, you can't have a sentence or a question without a verb! So, let us begin with learning them.

In simple words, verbs are words that describe:

- an action such as *run, sleep, shout* (action verbs)
- state of being such as *think, hear, see, smell, feel, love, hate, have, be* (stative verb)

Interesting Fact: Words that are used as verbs can be nouns too depending on how they are used in a sentence.

- I *love* her. (*Love* is a *verb* because it indicates a state of being.)

  Love is in the air. (*Love* is a *noun* because it is a subject.)

- I *run* every day. (*Run* is a *verb* because it indicates an action.)

  Running is my favourite activity. (*Running* is a *noun* because it indicates the name of an activity.)

Tenses

Most of the errors with verbs are made because of using them in the wrong tense. So let's understand tenses thoroughly.

See the conversation between angry Richard and Angela about shouting in all the tenses.

Simple Tense

Present	Past	Future
Angela: What do you do every day?	**Angela:** What did you do yesterday/last year?	**Angela:** What will you do tomorrow/next year?
Richard: I *shout* every day.	**Richard:** I *shouted* yesterday/last year.	**Richard:** I *will shout* tomorrow/next year.
Use this tense while describing a habit or general truth.	Use this tense for something you did in the past.	Use this tense for something you will do in the future.

Continuous Tense

Present	Past	Future
Angela: What are you doing?	**Angela:** What were you doing?	**Angela:** What will you be doing when I reach?
Richard: I *am talking* to you.	**Richard:** I *was shouting* before you called.	**Richard:** I *will be shouting* when you reach.
Use this tense while describing something you are doing at the time of talking.	Use this tense while describing something you did for a while but could not complete.	Use this tense while describing something you will be doing at some time in the future.

Perfect Tense

Present	Past	Future
Angela: What have you done?	**Angela:** What had you done when I reached?	**Angela:** What will you have done when I reach?
Richard: I *have shouted* at him.	**Richard:** I *had shouted* at him when you reached.	**Richard:** I *will have shouted* at him when you reach.
Use this tense while describing something you started and has continued till now and finished.	Use this tense while describing something you completed in the past before another event took place.	Use this tense while describing something you will complete before another event takes place.

Perfect Continuous Tense

Present	Past	Future
Angela: What have you been doing in the last few hours?	**Angela:** What had you been doing when I reached?	**Angela:** What will you have been doing when I reach?
Richard: I *have been shouting* at him in the last few hours.	**Richard:** I *had been shouting* at him when you reached.	**Richard:** I *will have been shouting* at him when you reach.
Use this tense while describing something you started at some point in the past and may or may not be complete.	Use this tense while describing something you did in the past and continued till that time.	Use this tense while describing something you will do for some time but not complete before another event takes place.

Activity

1. Fill up the charts below using the verb, *laugh*.
2. Spend some time on filling the chart carefully as it can get very difficult to communicate in English correctly if we don't use the correct tense.
3. Check the answers once you are done.

Simple Tense

Present	Past	Future
Angela: What do you do every day?	**Angela:** What did you do yesterday/ last year?	**Angela:** What will you do tomorrow/ next year?
You:	**You:**	**You:**

Continuous Tense

Present	Past	Future
Angela: What are you doing? **You:**	**Angela:** What were you doing? **You:**	**Angela:** What will you be doing when I reach? **You:**

Perfect Tense

Present	Past	Future
Angela: What have you done? **You:**	**Angela:** What had you done when I reached? **You:**	**Angela:** What will you have done when I reach? **You:**

Perfect Continuous Tense

Present	Past	Future
Angela: What have you been doing in the last few hours? **You:**	**Angela:** What had you been doing when I reached? **You:**	**Angela:** What will you have been doing when I reach? **You:**

Answers

Simple Tense

Present	Past	Future
Angela: What do you do every day? **You:** I *laugh* every day. Use this tense while describing a habit or general truth.	**Angela:** What did you do yesterday/last year? **You:** I *laughed* yesterday/last year. Use this tense for something you did in the past.	**Angela:** What will you do tomorrow/next year? **You:** I *will laugh* tomorrow/next year. Use this tense for something you will do in the future.

Continuous Tense

Present	Past	Future
Angela: What are you doing? **You:** I *am laughing* at you. Use this tense while describing something you are doing at the time of talking.	**Angela:** What were you doing? **You:** I *was laughing* before you called. Use this tense while describing something you did for a while but could not complete.	**Angela:** What will you be doing when I reach? **You:** I *will be laughing* when you reach. Use this tense while describing something you will be doing at some time in the future.

Perfect Tense

Present	Past	Future
Angela: What have you done? **You:** I *have laughed* at him. Use this tense while describing something you started and has continued till now and finished.	**Angela:** What had you done when I reached? **You:** I *had laughed* at him when you reached. Use this tense while describing something you completed in the past before another event took place.	**Angela:** What will you have done when I reach? **You:** I *will have laughed* at him when you reach. Use this tense while describing something you will complete before another event takes place.

Perfect Continuous Tense

Present	Past	Future
Angela: What have you been doing in the last few hours? **You:** I *have been laughing* at him in the last few hours. Use this tense while describing something you started at some point in the past and may or may not be complete.	**Angela:** What had you been doing when I reached? **You:** I *had been laughing* at him when you reached. Use this tense while describing something you did in the past and continued till that time.	**Angela:** What will you have been doing when I reach? **You:** I *will have been laughing* at him when you reach. Use this tense while describing something you will do for some time but not complete before another event takes place.

Stative Verbs

Now that you understand action verbs, let's discuss stative verbs. Verbs that describe a state of being rather than action. They could be thoughts, emotions, or senses.

Common Errors

A very common error is to use these verbs in the continuous tense. These verbs are not usually used with *-ing*. We use them in simple tenses.

- The food *is smelling* good. (Wrong)
  The food *smells* good. (Right)

- I *am loving* the feedback he gave me. (Wrong)
  I *love* the feedback he gave me. (Right)

- I *am feeling* that you are at fault. (Wrong)
  I *feel* that you are at fault. (Right)

- I *am hearing* you. (Wrong)
  I *hear* you. (Right)

- Are you *understanding* me? (Wrong)
  Can you *understand* me? (Right)

- I *am having* fever. (Wrong)
  I *have* fever. (Right)

Interesting Fact: Sometimes stative verb are used in the *–ing* form. Notice that their meaning changes.

- I *am having* food. (Right because here it means eating.)
- I *am hearing* voices. (Right because here it means imagining.)
- Rahul *is seeing* her. (Right because here it means dating.)

Now, take a look at the sentences below. They are all correct.

- I get a *feeling* that she is kind.
- *Hating* her won't help you.
- You need to do some focussed *thinking* before you take a decision.

Note: In the sentences above, the words in italics are not verbs; they are used as nouns as they describe an activity. Remember, nouns are words that describe a name, place, thing, or activity. Such words are called **gerunds**.

Gerunds are verb + ing.

Let's review some examples of gerunds with action verbs.

- I like to *dance*. (Dance is a verb.)

  Dancing is my hobby. (Dancing is a gerund.)

- I *help* them. (Help is a verb.)

  I look forward to *helping* them. (Helping is a gerund.)

- I *replied* when I was ready. (Reply is a verb.)

  I remember *replying* when I was ready. (Replying is a gerund.)

Activity

1. Create two sentences using stative verbs (without using them in an *ing* form).
2. Create two sentences using gerunds (*verb + ing*).

Stative Verbs

Have: _________________

Hear: _________________

Gerunds

Writing: _________________

Communicating: _______

Regular and Irregular Verbs

We normally convert verbs into past tense by adding a –d, -ed, or –ied.

- Laugh-laughed
- Shout-shouted
- Play-played
- Dance-danced
- Rain-rained

Such verbs are **regular verbs**. However, verbs that cannot be converted into past tense by adding a –d, -ed, or –ied are called **irregular verbs**.

- Let-let
- Hold-held
- Cut-cut
- Sell-sold

Brainstorm: List five more irregular verbs with their past tense.

Auxiliary or Helping Verbs

As the name suggests, **auxiliary** or **helping verbs** are used with the main verb to show the verb's tense. Remember when we made sentences for various tenses, we used *am*, *was*, *be*, and *have*. These are helping verbs.

Three common helping verbs are:

- Have
- Be
- Do

Let's discuss each of these.

Have: We used *have* and its forms in sentences and questions while learning tenses. See the underlined words in the table.

Perfect Tense

Present	Past	Future
Angela: What <u>have</u> you done? **Richard:** I *have shouted* at him.	**Angela:** What <u>had</u> you done when I reached? **Richard:** I *had shouted* at him when you reached.	**Angela:** What will you <u>have</u> done when I reach? **Richard:** I *will have shouted* at him when you reach.

Perfect Continuous Tense

Present	Past	Future
Angela: What <u>have</u> you been doing in the last few hours? **Richard:** I *have been shouting* at him in the last few hours.	**Angela:** What <u>had</u> you been doing when I reached? **Richard:** I *had been shouting* at him when you reached.	**Angela:** What will you <u>have</u> been doing when I reach? **Richard:** I *will have been shouting* at him when you reach.

Forms of *have*: have, has, had

Be: We used *be* in sentences and questions while learning tenses. See the underlined words. *Is, was, were, am, are, been* are all forms of *be*.

Continuous Tense

Present	Past	Future
Angela: What <u>are</u> you doing? **Richard:** I *am talking* to you.	**Angela:** What <u>were</u> you doing? **Richard:** I *was shouting* before you called.	**Angela:** What will you <u>be</u> doing when I reach? **Richard:** I *will be shouting* when you reach.

Perfect Continuous Tense

Present	Past	Future
Angela: What have you <u>been</u> doing in the last few hours?	**Angela:** What had you <u>been</u> doing when I reached?	**Angela:** What will you have <u>been</u> doing when I reach?
Richard: I *have* <u>*been*</u> *shouting* at him in the last few hours.	**Richard:** I *had* <u>*been*</u> *shouting* at him when you reached.	**Richard:** I *will have* <u>*been*</u> *shouting* at him when you reach.

Forms of *be*: is, am are, was, were, been

Do: We did not use *do* as a helping verb while learning tenses. We used it as the main verb. Let me give you a few examples of how *do* is used as a helping verb.

- I *do* like him.
- He *did* complete the work.
- She *does* think that English is important.

Do has a very common usage while confirming something.

- I like him, *don't* I?
- He completed the homework, *didn't* he?
- She thinks that English is important, *doesn't* she?

Interesting Fact: Helping verbs can be used as main verbs too.

- Bob *is* a good boy. (Is – main verb)
- I am *having* coffee. (Have – main verb; am – helping verb)
- I am *done* with the work. (Done – main verb, am – helping verb)

Modals

A modal is a type of helping verb. They are used with the main verb to express: ability, permission, obligation, possibility, advice, and prohibition.

For example, *can, could, may, might, must, shall, should, will, would.*

Since they are helping verbs, they are obviously going to be used with a main verb.

Points to Remember

1. A modal is always followed by the base form of a verb when used in sentences.
   - He *can* study.
   - He *could* study.
   - He *may* study.
   - He *must* study.
   - He *shall* study.
   - He *should* study.
   - He *will* study.
   - He *would* study.

2. A modal will **not** be followed by the word *to*.
   - He *can to* study. (Wrong)
   - He *could to* study. (Wrong)
   - He *may to* study. (Wrong)
   - He *must to* study. (Wrong)
   - He *shall to* study. (Wrong)
   - He *should to* study. (Wrong)
   - He *will to* study. (Wrong)
   - He *would to* study. (Wrong)

Confusing Part: Which modal to use when?

Different modals can be used in a sentence. Their usage would change the meaning of the sentence.

- What is the difference between *can* and *could*?
  - He *can* study. (**Means:** He has the ability to study.)
  - He *could* study. (**Means:** He had the ability to study in the past. He *could* study when he was younger.)
- What is the difference between *may* and *must*?
  - He *may* study. (**Means:** There is a possibility that he will study.)
  - He *must* study. (**Means:** He needs to study, it is very important for him.)
- What is the difference between *shall* and *should*?
  - He *shall* study. (**Means:** It's a mandate for him to study; he has no option but to study.)
  - He *should* study. (**Means:** It's an advice that he should study.)
- What is the difference between *will* and *would*?
  - He *will* study. (**Means:** He will definitely study.)
  - He *would* study. (**Means:** There is a possibility that he will study but it's not a guarantee.)

Let's get more clarity on modals through this passage.

There was a time when Ana *could* run fast. As of today, she *can* run but not as fast as she *used to*. She *may* run tomorrow but she *must* practise if she wants to win. The judges *shall* eliminate all those who run slowly. I feel she *should* start practising right now. I also believe that she *will* win if she listens to me. The judges *would* notice her.

Interesting Fact: *Used to* is a modal. It also follows the same rule, that is, it cannot be followed by the word *to*. It already has the word *to* in it. It is used to indicate something that happened continuously or frequently during a period in the past.

Activity

1. Fill out the following passage using these modals: *can, could, shall, should, used to, may, must, will, would.*

2. Use each modal only once.

3. Check the answers.

4. Review the notes given above if you get confused.

I know John____write. He
_________________________________ complete English exercises
in seconds. If he _____________________________ do it then,
what is the issue today? He _____________________________ ask
for some practice time but you _____________________________
trust his ability to write. You _____________________________
regret if you don't hire John for this assignment.
You_____________________________ think over it. You
_____________________________lose out on a good candidate.
We _____________________________ discuss further after his
interview.

Answers

I know John *can* write. He *used to* complete English exercises in seconds. If he *could* do it then, what is the issue today? He *may* ask for some practice time but you *must* trust his ability to write. You *will* regret if you don't hire John for this assignment. You *should* think over it. You *would* lose out on a good candidate. We *shall* discuss further after his interview.

Phrasal Verbs

A phrasal verb = a verb + a preposition, for example, get up. (*Get* is the verb and *up* is the preposition.)

We haven't covered prepositions yet, but one key point to remember is that phrasal verbs work just like normal verbs when used in sentences. So if we use them in the present tense, we will use *get up* and if we use them in the past tense, we will use *got up*.

- They *get up* at 6 am. (Present tense)

  They *got up* at 6 am. (Past tense)

- This car always *breaks down*. (Present tense)

  This car *broke down* yesterday. (Past tense)

Some more examples: *wake up, get out, take off, cheer up*.

Activity

Make sentences with the phrasal verbs given below. An example is given for your reference.

Woke up: I woke up pretty late.

Cheer up: Cheer me up, please.

Take off: Take off your shoes before you enter the house.

Get out: If you don't get out of the room, I will call the police.

Common Errors Related to Verb Usage

- There are some verbs that should not be followed by prepositions and some verbs that need a preposition. Rather than remembering more rules, review the following examples and use these verbs correctly. You will adapt to using verbs correctly as you communicate more and more in English. Alternatively, keep watching English movies or programmes to increase your vocabulary.

Wrong	Right
I will *propose* her.	I will *propose to* her.
She *told to* me.	She *told* me.

Wrong	Right
She *said* me.	She *said to* me.
We *discussed about* what happened in his meeting.	We *discussed* what happened in his meeting.

- Using double past tense is wrong, for example:

Wrong	Right
I *didn't got* you.	I *didn't get* you.
She *didn't understood*.	She *didn't understand*.
He *didn't helped* her.	He *didn't help* her.
I *did finished* the work.	I *did finish* the work.

Passive Voice

Since we are learning verbs, it's a good idea to know about passive voice too. Normally, a subject does an action to an object, for example, *Mary borrowed the book.*

If we say this in passive voice, it becomes, *The book was borrowed by Mary.*

In passive voice, we stress on the action (the verb) and the object of a sentence rather than subject.

Some more examples:

- Rita cleaned her house. (Active voice)

  Her house was cleaned by Rita. (Passive voice)

- Tom gave her that gift. (Active voice)

  That gift was given to her by Tom. (Passive voice)

Remember, do not speak in passive voice unless absolutely necessary. Active voice is clearer and crisp. People who use too much passive voice can sound very boring. Take a look at the example below and think what is better:

Raju proposing to his girlfriend in passive voice

I promise you will be loved by me. If my proposal is accepted, you will always be taken care of by me.

Raju proposing to his girlfriend in active voice

I promise I will I love you. If you accept, I will always take care of you.

And guess what, the girlfriend ran away when Raju proposed to her in passive voice. People will understand and believe in you more if you use active voice.

Then why are we learning passive voice?

- So that we consciously avoid using it.
- So that we understand its correct usage. The passive is often used to report something or when we don't know who the subject is, for example:
  - The market will be closed tomorrow.
  - Both the items were shipped by their company.

Listening Activity

In this chapter, we have covered a variety of errors made while using verbs. Given below is a list of the errors we discussed along with what is right.

1. Read the wrong sentence loudly without looking at the correct one.
2. Correct it verbally and check to see if you are right.
3. Repeat the process for all the sentences.
4. Refer to the notes in the chapter if you get stuck.

Wrong	Right
I drived yesterday.	I *drove* yesterday.
I putted the book in the cupboard yesterday.	I *put* the book in the cupboard yesterday.
I shift my house five years ago.	I *shifted* to a new house five years ago.
I will study yesterday.	I *studied* yesterday. I will study *tomorrow*.
The food is smelling good.	The food *smells* good.
I am loving the feedback he gave me.	I *love* the feedback he gave me.
I am feeling that you are at fault.	I *feel* that you are at fault.
I am hearing you.	I *hear* you.
Are you understanding me?	Can you *understand* me?
I am having fever.	I *have* fever.
She holded my hand.	She *held* my hand.
He thinked in English.	He *thought* in English.
I do liked him.	I *do like* him. I *did like* him.
He can to study.	He *can* study.
I will propose her.	I will *propose to* her.
She told to me.	She *told* me.
She said me.	She *said to* me.
We discussed about what happened in his meeting.	We *discussed* what happened in his meeting.
I didn't got you.	I *didn't get* you.
She didn't understood.	She *didn't understand*.
He didn't helped her.	He *didn't help* her.
I did finished the work.	I *did finish* the work.

Self-Practice Activity

Using verbs correctly requires practice.

Practice Option 1

1. Stand in front of a mirror and speak on each of the following topics in English for at least a minute.
   a. My Childhood
   b. My Hobbies
   c. My Future Plans
2. Record yourself when you do this.
3. Make a good speaker of English language listen to your recording.
4. Ask for feedback on grammar and pronunciation.

Practice Option 2

1. Stand in front of a mirror and speak on each of the following topics in English for at least a minute.
   a. My Childhood
   b. My Hobbies
   c. My Future Plans
2. Make a good speaker of English language listen to you when you speak.
3. Ask for feedback on grammar and pronunciation.

In case you don't have someone to give you feedback, then try to recognize your own errors by speaking slowly.

Learning Tips

- Pick as many simple free speech topics as you can and speak on them for a minute. Do not start writing about them. The idea is to get conversational.

- Think and speak in English as much as you can.
- Review the common errors made while using verbs at least once a week.
- Do not speak incorrectly if you hear others speak incorrectly. Get into the habit of identifying errors.
- Whenever you get confused while using verbs, review the notes again.
- Make a note of anything new that you discover related to verbs in the section below.

Personal Notes

____

____

____

____

Pronunciation Time

Say the following word aloud: *assign*.

If we break it into sounds, we hear the following sounds in two parts: (uh)/s(ai)n. Each part is called a **syllable**.

Refer to these charts to recall the symbols for the sounds.

Consonant Sounds Chart	
Unvoiced	**Voiced**
p (pen)	**b** (bet)
k (kite)	**g** (gate)
t (time)	**d** (date)
f (fox)	**v** (voucher)
s (strand)	**z** (zebra)
th (theory)	**th**(e) (father)
sh (shoe)	**zh** (treasure)

Consonant Sounds Chart	
Unvoiced	**Voiced**
ch (chicken)	**j** (jet)
h (hen)	**l** (lane)
	m (mat)
	n (nose)
	ng (ring)
	r (car)
	w (water)
	y (Yugoslavia)

Vowel Sounds Chart	
Long	**Short**
ay (they)	**ae** (that)
ee (she)	**eh** (them)
ai (mine)	**ih** (it)
oh (both)	**aw** (all)
oo (you)	**o** (book) – Book is a noun.
ew (few)	**uh** (us) – schwa
aa (car) – Car is a noun.	
Schwa followed by the letter R	
er (her)	
Diphthongs	
oy (boy) – Boy is a noun. (Made by combining aw and ay.)	
ow (cow) – Cow is a noun. (Made by combining aa and oh.)	

You will be learning syllables in the Pronunciation section.

Learning Tip: Before we begin syllables, I recommend that you practise saying the consonant and vowel sounds aloud along with examples.

We form a **syllable** when we combine consonant sounds with a vowel sound.

Characteristics of a Syllable

- Each syllable has a vowel sound. Therefore, one vowel sound indicates the word has one syllable, two vowel sounds indicate the word has two syllables, and so on. The word *assign* has two vowel sounds, and hence, two syllables.
- A vowel sound alone can be a syllable but a consonant sound alone cannot be a syllable. Let's take an example.
  - In the word, *alone*, there are two syllables: uh and l(oh)n.
  - Note that (uh) is a vowel sound and can be a syllable on its own.
- In a word, **only one** syllable is stressed. While pronouncing very long words, you may feel that you are stressing more than one syllable. However, the secondary stress is very little.
- Only vowel sounds are stressed, not consonant sounds.

Activity

1. Open an online dictionary on your computer.
2. Search for the word *assign*.
3. Notice that the stressed syllable is indicated by an apostrophe right before the stressed syllable. In the word *assign*, the second syllable is stressed.
4. Listen to the pronunciation and say the word aloud.

Why is Syllable Stress Important?

You will not be able to pronounce a word correctly if you do not stress the right syllable. Sometimes, a word can change its meaning if you stress the wrong syllable. You will learn this as you proceed.

Learning Tips

- When you break a word into syllables, only focus on the sounds, not the spelling.
- For ease of learning, we will break the words without using symbols. For example:
  - Instead of breaking the word *assign* into (uh)/s(ai)n, we will simply break it as as/sign keeping the sound in mind.
  - We will highlight the stressed syllable: as/**sign**.
- Keep an online dictionary opened while reviewing this chapter as you will need to listen to the pronunciation of words to identify the stressed syllable.
- Raise your hand while you stress a syllable. It helps in stressing the syllable correctly as your body language supports what you are saying.
- Stress the syllable by raising your volume and pitch and stressing the vowel sound in that syllable.

Syllable Stress Rules

There are rules to syllable stress that help us identify the stressed syllable in a word. Some of them have hundred percent accuracy and some have exceptions. Also, there are a plenty of rules. We will review a few that we can remember easily.

You will automatically start pronouncing words correctly if you get into a habit of checking the pronunciation of a word as well as checking the stressed syllable using an online dictionary whenever you are unsure of how it is pronounced.

Words may also differ in pronunciation due to the differences in British and American accent. If you come across a word that can be pronounced in different ways, choose the one you find easier.

Activity

1. Review the rules below.
2. Listen to the pronunciation of the words using an online dictionary.
3. Identify the stressed syllable.
4. Say the word aloud while raising your hand when you stress the syllable.
5. Stress the syllable by raising your volume and pitch and stressing the vowel sound in that syllable.

Rule 1: Noun and Verb Rule

If a word has two syllables, we stress the first syllable when it is used as a noun and we stress the second syllable when it is used as a verb, for example:

The **ob**ject is shiny. (Noun)

I ob**ject** to what you said. (Verb)

Note: The meaning of a word can change with a change in syllable stress.

Examples:

object (Noun) – object (Verb)

project (Noun) – pro**ject** (Verb)

record (Noun) – **re**cord (Verb)

import (Noun) – import (Verb)

export (Noun) – ex**port** (Verb)

contrast (Noun) – con**trast** (Verb)

reject (Noun) – re**ject** (Verb)

conduct (Noun) – con**duct** (Verb)

present (Noun) – pre**sent** (Verb)

Rule 2: Words ending in

- er
- ly

We stress the first syllable in the word.

Examples:

easier, **ang**rier, **hap**pier, **hea**vier

easily, **ang**rily, **hap**pily, **hea**vily

Rule 3: Words ending in

- tion
- sion
- ic

We stress the second syllable from the end of the word.

Examples:

communication, pronunciation

decision, precision

economic, electronic

Rule 4: Words ending in

- cy
- ty
- gy
- phy
- al

We stress the third syllable from the end of the word.

Examples:

de**mo**cracy, **a**gency

ca**la**mity, re**a**lity

ge**o**logy, a**stro**logy

ge**o**graphy, pho**to**graphy

logical, philo**so**phical

Rule 5: Words ending in

- able
- ial
- cian
- ish
- ious
- ient
- ery

We stress the syllable before the ending.

Examples:

pre**sen**table, a**do**rable

arti**fi**cial, bene**fi**cial

mu**si**cian, elec**tri**cian

snobbish, **Eng**lish

precious, hi**la**rious

gradient, **pa**tient

gallery, **bat**tery

Rule 6: Words ending in

- ade
- ee

- oon
- que
- eer
- ette

We usually stress the ending.

Examples:

lemo**nade**

guaran**tee**

after**noon**

bou**tique**

volun**teer**

ciga**rette**

Rule 7: Compound Nouns

Remember compound nouns that are made up of two or more words?

While saying these nouns, we stress the first word.

Examples: Keyboard, **Pen** stand

Rule 8: Phrasal Verbs

Remember phrasal verbs that are made up of verb + preposition?

While saying these verbs, we stress the second word, that is, the preposition.

Examples: get **up**, wake **up**

Rule 9: Proper Nouns

Remember proper nouns that are names of people, places, or things?

While saying these nouns, we stress the second word.

Examples:

Mr. **Ahuja**

North **America**

Microsoft **Corporation**

Rule 10: Reflexive Pronouns

Remember these are objects that refer to the subject?

While saying these pronouns, we stress the second syllable.

Examples:

my**self**

him**self**

her**self**

them**selves**

Rule 11: Acronyms

An acronym is a pronounceable word that is formed using the first letters of the words in a phrase, for example:

- LASER - **Light** a**mplification** **by** the **stimulated** **emission** of **radiation.**
- NASA - **National Aeronautics and Space Administration**

While saying these acronyms, we usually stress the first syllable.

Examples:

LASER

NASA

Rule 12: Initialisms

An initialism is a word that is formed using the first letters of the words in a phrase, for example:

- UFO: **Unidentified Flying Object**
- MBA: **Master of Business Administration**

While saying these Initialisms, we usually stress the last syllable.

Rule 13: Numbers ending in teen

We stress the second syllable. fif**teen**, six**teen**, seven**teen**, eigh**teen.**

When the -teen number is used as an adjective (when it describes a noun), we stress the first syllable.

As an adjective, we say:

A **six**teen cm thick book.

An **eigh**teen inch long rope.

Rule 14: Numbers that are multiples of ten:

We stress the first syllable.

Examples:

twenty, **thir**ty, **fif**ty, **six**ty, **one**-hundred, **two**-hundred

Learning Tips

- If you apply the syllable stress rules while communicating in English, you will see an instant change in the way you speak. Let me remind you that it needs practise and conscious effort to pronounce words correctly.
- Make it a habit to check the pronunciation of a word as well the stressed syllable using an online dictionary whenever you are unsure of how it is pronounced. This way you will remember it throughout your life.
- Raise your hand while you stress a syllable. It helps in stressing the syllable correctly as your body language supports what you are saying.
- Stress the syllable by raising your volume and pitch and stressing the vowel sound in that syllable.

- Open your mouth as much as you can while practising pronunciation. A lot of times we sound unclear because we don't open our mouth enough while speaking.

Activity

1. Listen to the pronunciation of days and months using an online dictionary.
2. Identify the stressed syllable. It is also given below for you reference.
3. Say them aloud while raising your hand when you stress the syllable.
4. Stress the syllable by raising your volume and pitch and stressing the vowel sound in that syllable.

Common Error

Many people mispronounce Wednesday. It has only two syllables: **wenz**-day.

Days	Months
• **Mon**day	• **Jan**uary
• **Tues**day	• **Feb**ruary
• **Wednes**day	• **March**
• **Thurs**day	• **April**
• **Fri**day	• **May**
• **Sat**urday	• **June**
• **Sun**day	• **July**
	• **August**
	• Sep**tem**ber
	• Oc**to**ber
	• No**vem**ber
	• De**cem**ber

Self-Practice Activity

Pronouncing words correctly requires practice. The following activities will help you improve throughout life.

Activity 1

1. Pick up a simple English book and read it aloud.
2. Focus on pronouncing vowel sounds, consonant sounds and syllables correctly. This will automatically make you pronounce words correctly.
3. Make a good speaker of English language listen to you when you speak.
4. Ask for feedback on Pronunciation.

Note: If you don't find someone to listen to you instantly, record yourself and send the recording for evaluation to someone who is good at English. Ask for feedback on Pronunciation.

Activity 2

1. Learn pronouncing a new word each day.
2. Search for words you find difficult or names you cannot pronounce. Find out the sounds and syllables in them.
3. Write them in the space below.
4. Practise them by saying the sounds correctly and stressing the right syllable.

New Words

Self-Practice Activity

Watch another English movie or a programme on T.V. to get used to understanding English.

Now you can go back to the video game or wish list table given in Chapter 1 and tick Verbs and Syllables.

Chapter 5

• • • • • • • • • •

SUBJECT VERB AGREEMENT, QUESTION FORMATION, SENTENCE STRESS AND INTONATION

Do you remember this formula from the previous chapters?

What Is a Sentence Made Up of?

Sentence = Subject + Verb + Object.

To speak correctly, the subject needs to agree with the verb. A lot of errors occur while communicating in English when we use the wrong form of the verb with a subject.

Therefore, let us begin with learning Subject Verb Agreement.

Recall

- Which words are used as subjects?

  Usually nouns and pronouns.

- What are nouns?

  People, places, things, occasions, ideas, feelings, state of being, for example, boy, book, country, United Kingdom, love, education, birthday.

- What are pronouns?

  Words that replace nouns, for example, I, you, he, she, we and they.

- What are verbs?

  - Action verbs: words that show action, for example, run, dance, laugh, write.
  - Stative verbs: Words that describe state of being, for example, love, think, hear, feel, have.

Interesting Fact

Note that the word *love* can be a noun or a verb depending on how it used in a sentence.

- He *loves* her. (Love is a verb.)
- *Love* is a beautiful feeling. (Love is an abstract noun.)

Subject Verb Agreement Rules

Take a look at the diagram below.

The basic rule of subject verb agreement is: A singular subject has a singular verb and a plural subject has a plural verb.

For example:

- *Rahul plays* football. (*Rahul* is a singular subject; therefore, we have used a singular verb, *plays*.)

- *Rahul* and *Teena play* football. (*Rahul* and *Teena* together form a plural subject; therefore, we have used a plural verb, *play*.)

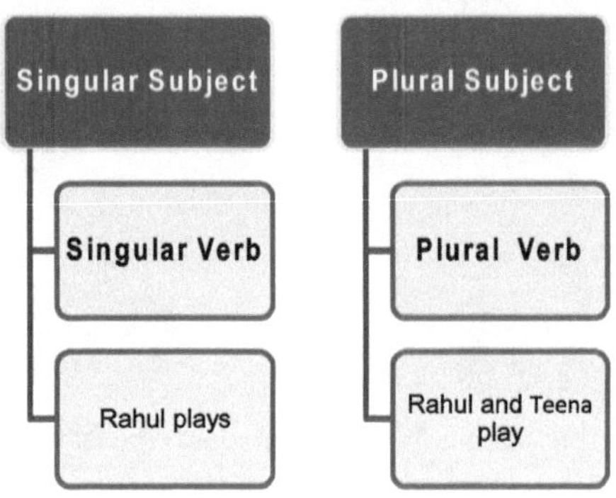

Singular and Plural Forms of Verbs

In the examples above, note:

- The singular form of the verb is made by adding an s in the end (*plays*)
- The plural form is without the s (play)

Keeping the above rules in mind, let's change the following verbs into singular and plural forms.

Verb	Singular Form	Plural Form
think	thinks	think
jump	jumps	jump
give	gives	give
take	takes	take
write	writes	write

Take a look at the following chart with the verb *eat* as an example. Notice that the singular subjects have a singular verb and the plural subjects have a plural verb, except for *I* and *You*. We use a plural verb with *I* and *You*.

	Noun as a subject	Pronoun as a subject
Singular		
First person	Reema <u>eats</u>.	I <u>eat</u>.
Second person	Shreya <u>eats</u>.	You <u>eat</u>.
Third person	Rosy <u>eats</u>.	He, She, It <u>eats</u>.
Plural		
First person	Reema and her friend <u>eat</u>.	We <u>eat</u>.
Second person	Shreya and her friend <u>eat</u>.	You <u>eat</u>.
Third person	Rosy and her friend <u>eat</u>.	They <u>eat</u>.

Activity

1. Fill up the chart below using the verb, *walk*.
2. Check the answers once you are done.

	Noun as a subject	Pronoun as a subject
Singular		
First person	Reema ___________	I ___________
Second person	Shreya ___________	You ___________
Third person	Rosy ___________	He, She, It ___________
Plural		
First person	Reema and her friend ___________	We ___________
Second person	Shreya and her friend ___________	You ___________
Third person	Rosy and her friend ___________	They ___________

Answers

	Noun as a subject	**Pronoun as a subject**
Singular		
First person	Reema <u>walks</u>.	I <u>walk</u>.
Second person	Shreya <u>walks</u>.	You <u>walk</u>.
Third person	Rosy <u>walks</u>.	He, She, It <u>walks</u>.
Plural		
First person	Reema and her friend <u>walk</u>.	We <u>walk</u>.
Second person	Shreya and her friend <u>walk</u>.	You <u>walk</u>.
Third person	Rosy and her friend <u>walk</u>.	They <u>walk</u>.

We have understood the basic rule of subject verb agreement, that is, *a singular subject has a singular verb and a plural subject has a plural verb.*

Let's review more rules. We will only cover a few that are essential. If you apply these correctly, the rest of the rules will automatically fall in place.

Rule 1

In longer sentences, many words come between the subject and the verb. If the subject is singular, use a singular verb and if the subject is plural, use a plural verb.

- The **man**, who reads many books, loves writing. (*Man* is singular; hence, <u>*loves*</u> is singular.)
- The **men**, who read many books, <u>love</u> writing. (*Men* is plural; hence, *love* is plural.)
- The **bag** full of flowers <u>smells</u> great. (*Bag* is singular; hence, *smells* is singular.)

Rule 2

When sentences start with "there" or "here," always place the main subject after the verb.

- There <u>are</u> **candles** in the room. (*Candles* is the main subject, it is placed after the verb, *are*. *Candles* is plural; hence, *are* is plural.)
- There <u>is</u> a good **chance** of learning English. (*Chance* is the main subject, it is placed after the verb, *is*. *Chance* is plural; hence, *is* is plural.)

Rule 3

If two subjects are joined by *and,* you will typically use a plural verb form.

- **Rohan** and **Shashank** <u>are</u> good people. (The subjects *Rohan* and *Shashank* are joined by *and*; hence, a plural verb, *are*.)
- The **book** and the **pen** <u>are</u> black. (The subjects *book* and *pen* are joined by *and*; hence, a plural verb form, *are*.)

Rule 4

If two subjects are separated by *and* but they refer to one thing, you will use a singular verb form. These are more like compound nouns and hence are considered as one subject.

- **Curry and rice** <u>makes</u> a great meal. (In this sentence, *curry and rice* represents one meal; hence, a singular verb, *makes*.)
- **Red and black** <u>is</u> my favourite colour combination. (In this sentence, *red and black* represents one combination; hence, a singular verb, *is*.)

Rule 5

Indefinite pronouns can be singular or plural. When they are singular, use a singular verb. When they are plural, use a plural verb.

Remember, this was also covered in the Pronouns chapter.

Singular	Plural	Singular or Plural
somebody, someone, something, another, anybody, anyone, anything, each, either, neither, everybody, everyone, everything, little, much, no one, nobody, nothing, one, other	others, both, few, many, several	none, most, more, any, all, some
Examples		
Neither of the girls <u>is</u> polite.	**Many** of the girls <u>are</u> polite.	**All** of the people <u>are</u> good.
One of the boys <u>enjoys</u> reading.	**Few** of the boys <u>enjoy</u> reading.	**All** of the population <u>is</u> good.
Examples		
Everyone <u>wants</u> to speak well.	**Several** of them <u>want</u> to speak well.	**Most** of them <u>want</u> to speak well.

Rule 6

Collective nouns, uncountable nouns, and abstract nouns are usually singular. Therefore, use a singular verb form with them.

Uncountable
butter, cheese, honey, water, wood, rice, hair

Collective
army, group, band, team, village, school, bunch

<table>
<tr><td align="center">Abstract</td></tr>
</table>

Feeling: love, hate, anger, peace

State: pain, happiness, loyalty, compassion

Events: education, reality

Ideas: truth, faith, belief

- **Cheese** is my favourite.
- Your **hair** is nice.
- Their **team** is the best.
- The **school** is closed.
- The **truth** is always bitter.

Rule 7

If a sentence has the following words, use the verb as per the subject closest to it.

Or, Either/or, Neither/nor, Not only/but also

- Linda or **Tom** bakes the cake. (*Tom* is closest to the verb and is singular; hence, use a singular verb.)
- Either Linda or **her friends** are coming to the party. (*Friends* is closest to the verb and is plural; hence, use a plural verb.)
- Either her friends or **her boyfriend** is responsible for her victory. (*Boyfriend* is closest to the verb and is singular; hence, use a singular verb.)
- Neither Bob nor **his cousins** have a good record. (*Cousins* is closest to the verb and is plural; hence, use a plural verb.)
- Neither the cousins nor **Bob** is helpful. (*Bob* is closest to the verb and is singular; hence, use a singular verb.)
- Neither Betty nor **her husband** needs to work. (*Husband* is closest to the verb and is singular; hence, use a singular verb.)

- Her friends or **cousins** <u>are</u> invited. (*Cousins* is closest to the verb and is plural; hence, use a plural verb.)

- Not only Jerry but also his **friends** <u>are</u> cunning. (*Friends* is closest to the verb and is plural; hence, use a plural verb.)

Rule 8

If the subject is separated by the following words in a sentence, use the verb as per the main subject. Ignore these words.

along with, as well as, besides, not

- The **actor**, along with his fans, <u>is</u> going to arrive soon. (*Actor* is singular; hence, use a singular verb.)

- **Grammar**, as well as pronunciation, is important. (*Grammar* is singular; hence, use a singular verb.)

- **Markers**, along with a whiteboard, <u>are</u> needed to conduct the training. (*Markers* is plural; hence, use a plural verb.)

Rule 9

Use a singular verb with distances, periods of time, and sums of money when considered as a unit.

- **Four years** <u>is</u> a long time to spend on learning English.

- **Hundred dollars** <u>is</u> not enough for you to buy what you want.

- **Ten kilometres** <u>is</u> a long distance to cover without a car.

Listening Activity

1. Read the sentences loudly and decide which verb to use.

2. Choose the verb and check if you are right.

3. Refer to the subject verb agreement rules if you get stuck.

Harry do/does magic.
Harry and Sunny do/does magic.
The boy, who has two laptops, is/are a genius.
Girls, who own a house, is/are lucky.
Here is/are his shoes.
There is/are no water in the glass.
The bride and the groom look/looks happy.
The table and the chair is/are broken.
Bread and jam is/are tasty.
Everything confuses/confuse me these days.
Most of the people is/are educated.
Most of the population is/are educated.
One of the boys is/are laughing.
Honey is/are healthy.
The team has/have a good spirit.
The reality is/are painful.
My aunt or uncle is/are going to dance.
Neither my friend nor his cousins is/are fun loving.
Either you or your mother needs/need to cook.
Either Ronny or his sisters has/have the authority to sign the paper.
Sheela, along with her sons, is/are going for the movie.
Noun as well as verb is/are important.
Emails as well as phone calls is/are needed.
Not only fish but also its bones annoys/annoy me.
Ten years is/are a long time.
Seven pounds is/are too less to buy that item.
Eight kilograms is/are difficult to lose.

Answers

Harry <u>does</u> magic.
Harry and **Sunny** <u>do</u> magic.
The **boy**, who has two laptops, <u>is</u> a genius.
Girls, who own a house, <u>are</u> lucky.
Here <u>are</u> his shoes.
There <u>is</u> no water in the glass.
The **bride** and the **groom** <u>look</u> happy.
The **table** and the **chair** <u>are</u> broken.
Bread and jam <u>is</u> tasty.
Everything <u>confuses</u> me these days.
Most of the people <u>are</u> educated.
Most of the population <u>is</u> educated.
One of the boys <u>is</u> laughing.
Honey <u>is</u> healthy.
The **team** <u>has</u> a good spirit.
The **reality** <u>is</u> painful.
My aunt or **uncle** <u>is</u> going to dance.
Neither my friend nor his **cousins** <u>are</u> fun loving.
Either you or your **mother** <u>needs</u> to cook.
Either Ronny or his **sisters** <u>have</u> the authority to sign the paper.
Sheela, along with her sons, <u>is</u> going for the movie.
Noun as well as verb <u>is</u> important.
Emails as well as phone calls <u>are</u> needed.
Not only fish but also its **bones** <u>annoy</u> me.
Ten years <u>is</u> a long time.
Seven pounds <u>is</u> too less to buy that item.
Eight kilograms <u>is</u> difficult to lose.

Interesting Fact

When sentences contain helping verbs such as do, did, does, can, could, may, might and so on, the verb used with them is without an **s**.

Examples:

- Rahul *plays*. (Right)

  Rahul *does play*. (Right)

- Rahul and Teena *play*. (Right)

  Rahul and Teena *do play*. (Right)

Self-Practice Activity

1. Stand in front of a mirror and speak on each of the following topics in English for a minute. Be creative and form a story on the topics.

   a. Sarah loves to dance.

   b. John thinks a lot.

2. Make a good speaker of English language listen to you when you speak.

3. Ask for feedback on Grammar and Pronunciation.

Note: If you don't find someone to listen to you instantly, record yourself and send the recording for evaluation to someone who is good at English. Ask for feedback on Grammar and Pronunciation.

Learning Tips

- A great technique to avoid subject verb agreement errors is to identity if the subject is singular or plural sand use the verb accordingly. With a singular subject, use a singular verb and with a plural subject, use a plural verb

- Pick as many simple free speech topics as you can and speak on them for a minute. Do not start writing about them. The idea is to get conversational.
- Think and speak in English as much as you can.
- Do not speak incorrectly if you hear others speak incorrectly. Get into the habit of identifying errors.
- Make a note of sentences you get confused with the section below.

Personal Notes

____

____

____

____

Question Formation

Why do we ask questions?

- To get information
- To get to know someone
- To confirm something

Therefore, it's essential to ask them correctly.

Let's review question formation.

Question Words

Questions begin with a question word. Take a minute to write some words with which you normally begin your questions.

____

____

____

____

If we were to organise question words, we can say questions begin with words in the chart below.

Wh- words and How	Helping Verbs
<ul><li>What</li><li>When</li><li>Where</li><li>Who</li><li>Whom</li><li>Whose</li><li>Which</li><li>Why</li><li>How</li></ul>	<ul><li>Is, am are, was, were</li><li>Do, did, does</li><li>Have, has , had</li><li>Modals: can, could, may, shall, should, will, would</li></ul>

Open-Ended Questions

Questions that begin with *Wh- words and how* are called **open-ended questions**. These questions are asked to get detailed or lengthy responses.

Examples:

- Why do you fly?
- How will you cook rice?
- How can you shout?

Notice that the responses to the questions above are bound to be lengthy.

When should you ask open-ended questions?

- When you want to get a lot of information
- When you want to encourage someone to talk

How do you construct open-ended questions?

Do you remember this formula from the previous chapters?

Sentence = Subject + Verb + Object

When we create questions, we put the verb before of the subject.

Open-Ended Questions = Wh- word or how + helping verb + subject + main verb + object (if any)

Examples:

Wh- Word or How	Helping Verb	Subject	Main Verb	Object
Why	do	you	fly?	
How	will	you	cook	rice?
How	can	you	shout?	

Activity

1. Break up the following questions into the chart below to grasp better.

    a. How will you adjust?

    b. When does he leave the country?

2. Check the answers once you are done.

Wh- Word or How	Helping Verb	Subject	Main Verb	Object

Answers

Wh- Word or How	Helping Verb	Subject	Main Verb	Object
How	will	you	adjust?	
When	does	she	leave	the country?

Interesting Fact: There are questions that don't have helping verbs. In such cases, the main verb is used after the question word.

Wh- Word or How	Main Verb	Subject	Object
What	is	your	name?
Where	do	you	stay?

Note: The questions given above generate a short answer and there is a common confusion around whether to categorise them as open-ended or closed-ended questions. I categorise them as closed-ended questions because they usually end up in one-word answers.

- Teena
- Delhi

Points to Remember

- Don't miss the verb or helping verb when forming questions.

Wrong	Right
What your name?	What *is* your name?
What you like?	What *do* you like?
What you want to eat?	What *do* you want to eat?
Where you live?	Where *do* you live?
What you mean?	What *do* you mean?

- Don't place the question word in the end.

Wrong	Right
Your name what?	*What* is your name?
You like what?	*What* do you like?
You want to eat what?	*What* do you want to eat?
You live where?	*Where* do you live?

- Always place the verb or helping verb before the subject.

Wrong	Right
What you are doing?	What *are you* doing?

Wrong	Right
Where you are going?	Where *are you* going?
What you are saying?	What *are you* saying?

- Do not use the main verb with an **-s** when they are used with helping verbs.

Wrong	Right
When does she leaves the country?	When does she *leave* the country?
What does he wants?	What does he *want*?
What did she writes?	What did she *write*?
What do they thinks?	What do they *think*?

- Ask the question in the right tense.

Wrong	Right
What movie do you watch yesterday?	What movie *did* you watch yesterday?
What movie do you watch tomorrow?	What movie *will* you watch tomorrow?

- Do not use **-ed** with the main verb when it is used with helping verbs.

Wrong	Right
When did he called?	When did he *call*?
What did she asked?	What did she *ask*?

Activity

Remember this table from the tenses section?

1. Review the questions in all tenses.
2. Notice the following:

    a. All questions begin with a questions word.

    b. The verb or helping verb is before the subject.

    c. When the question has *did*, the main verb remains without **–s** and without **-ed**.

3. Form questions in all tenses in the next table using the verb *cook*. An example is given for your reference.

4. Check the answers.

Simple Tense

Present	Past	Future
Angela: What do you do every day?	**Angela:** What did you do yesterday/ last year?	**Angela:** What will you do tomorrow/ next year?
Richard: I *shout* every day.	**Richard:** I *shouted* yesterday/last year.	**Richard:** I *will shout* tomorrow/next year.

Continuous Tense

Present	Past	Future
Angela: What are you doing?	**Angela:** What were you doing?	**Angela:** What will you be doing when I reach?
Richard: I *am talking* to you.	**Richard:** I *was shouting* before you called.	**Richard:** I *will be shouting* when you reach.

Perfect Tense

Present	Past	Future
Angela: What have you done?	**Angela:** What had you done when I reached?	**Angela:** What will you have done when I reach?

Present	Past	Future
Richard: I *have shouted* at him.	**Richard:** I *had shouted* at him when you reached.	**Richard:** I *will have shouted* at him when you reach.

Perfect Continuous Tense

Present	Past	Future
Angela: What have you been doing in the last few hours? **Richard:** I *have been shouting* at him in the last few hours.	**Angela:** What had you been doing when I reached? **Richard:** I *had been shouting* at him when you reached.	**Angela:** What will you have been doing when I reach? **Richard:** I *will have been shouting* at him when you reach.

Form questions!

	Present	Past	Future
Simple	What does he cook?		
Continuous			
Perfect			
Perfect Continuous			

Answers

	Present	**Past**	**Future**
Simple	What does he cook?	What did he cook?	What will he cook?
Continuous	What is he cooking?	What was he cooking?	What will he be cooking?
Perfect	What has he cooked?	What had he cooked when you reached?	What will he have cooked when you reach?
Perfect Continuous	What has he been cooking in the last few hours?	What had he been cooking when you reached?	What will he have been cooking when you reach?

Closed-Ended Questions

Questions that begin with *helping verbs* are called **closed-ended questions**. These questions are asked to get a "yes" or "no" answer or a one word answer.

Examples:

- Do you like cheese?
- Is she a nice girl?
- Can he swim?
- Would you like tea or coffee?

Notice that the responses to the questions above are either "yes" or "no" or one word.

When should you ask closed-ended questions?

- When you want a short and quick response
- When you want to confirm something

How do you construct closed-ended questions?

There are usually no Wh-or how words in closed-ended questions. They begin with helping verbs.

Closed-Ended Questions = Helping verb + subject + main verb + object (if any)

Examples:

Helping Verb	Subject	Main Verb	Object
Do	you	fly?	
Will	you	cook	rice?
Can	you	shout?	
Does	he	like	her?

Activity

1. Break up the following questions into the chart below to grasp better.

    a. Do you like cheese?

    b. Can he swim?

2. Check the answers once you are done.

Helping Verb	Subject	Main Verb	Object

Answers

Helping Verb	Subject	Main Verb	Object
Do	you	like	cheese?
Can	he	swim?	

Points to Remember

- Don't miss the helping verb when forming closed-ended questions. Else, they will be statements, not questions.

Statement	Question
You like cheese.	*Do* you like cheese?
You want water.	*Do* you want water?

- Always place the helping verb at the beginning when forming closed-ended questions.

Wrong	Right
You can eat fish?	*Can you* eat fish?
He can sing?	*Can he* sing?

- Do not use the main verb with an **-s** when they are used with helping verbs.

Wrong	Right
Does he likes mangoes?	Does he *like* mangoes?
Does she speaks well?	Does she *speak* well?

- Ask the question in the right tense.

Wrong	Right
Do you watch a movie yesterday?	*Did* you watch a movie yesterday?
Do you watch a movie tomorrow?	*Will* you watch a movie tomorrow?

- Do not use **-ed** with the main verb when it is used with helping verbs.

Wrong	Right
Did he called?	Did he *call*?
Did she asked him to practise?	Did she *ask* him to practise?

Listening Activity

In this chapter, we have covered a variety of errors made while forming questions. Given below is a list of the errors we discussed along with what is right.

1. Say the wrong question loudly without looking at the correct one.
2. Correct it verbally and identify which type of question it is – open-ended or closed-ended.
3. Check to see if you are right.
4. Repeat the process for all the questions.
5. Refer to the notes in the chapter if you get stuck.

Wrong	Right	Question Type
What your name?	What *is* your name?	Closed-ended (one-word answer)
What you like?	What *do* you like?	Open-ended
What you want to eat?	What *do* you want to eat?	Open-ended (if the answer is lengthy)
Where you live?	Where *do* you live?	Closed-ended (one-word answer)
What you mean?	What *do* you mean?	Open-ended
Your name what?	*What* is your name?	Closed-ended (one-word answer)
You like what?	*What* do you like?	Open-ended
You want to eat what?	*What* do you want to eat?	Open-ended (if the answer is lengthy)
You live where?	*Where* do you live?	Closed-ended (one-word answer)
What you are doing?	What *are you* doing?	Open-ended

Wrong	Right	Question Type
Where you are going?	Where *are* *you* going?	Open-ended
What you are saying?	What *are you* saying?	Open-ended
When does she leaves the country?	When does she *leave* the country?	Closed-ended (one-word answer)
What does he wants?	What does he *want*?	Open-ended
What did she writes?	What did she *write*?	Open-ended
What do they thinks?	What do they *think*?	Open-ended
What movie do you watch yesterday?	What movie *did* you watch yesterday?	Closed-ended (one-word answer)
What movie do you watch tomorrow?	What movie *will* you watch tomorrow?	Closed-ended (one-word answer)
When did he called?	When did he *call*?	Closed-ended (one-word answer)
What did she asked?	What did she *ask*?	Open-ended
You like cheese?	*Do* you like cheese?	Closed-ended
You want water?	*Do* you want water?	Closed-ended
You can eat fish?	*Can you* eat fish?	Closed-ended
He can sing?	*Can he* sing?	Closed-ended
Does he likes mangoes?	Does he *like* mangoes?	Closed-ended

Wrong	Right	Question Type
Does she speaks well?	Does she *speak* well?	Closed-ended
Do you watch a movie yesterday?	*Did* you watch a movie yesterday?	Closed-ended
Do you watch a movie tomorrow?	*Will* you watch a movie tomorrow?	Closed-ended
Did he called?	Did he *call*?	Closed-ended
Did she asked him to practise?	Did she *ask* him to practise?	Closed-ended

Now that you have understood open-ended and closed-ended questions, let's take a look at question tags.

Questions Tags are often used in spoken English. They are avoided in written English. They are a way of keeping the other person involved in the conversation.

For example,

- He is right, isn't he?
- He is not right, is he?
- She speaks well, doesn't she?
- She doesn't speak well, does she?

How do you form question tags?

Rule 1: Add a negative tag to a positive statement, and add a positive tag to a negative statement.

He is right, (positive statement)	isn't he? (negative tag)
He is not right, (negative statement)	is he? (positive tag)
She speaks well, (positive statement)	doesn't she? (negative tag)

She doesn't speak well, (negative statement)	does she? (positive tag)

Rule 2: Always form the tag by using the helping verb in the statement.

He **is** right,	**isn't** he?
He **is not** right,	**is** he?
She **doesn't** speak well,	**does** she?

Rule 3: If there is no helping verb in the statement, use *do*, *does*, or *did* to form the tag.

She speaks well,	doesn't she?
You completed the work,	didn't you?
He likes her,	doesn't he?
They know the answer,	don't they?

Activity

1. Add question tags to the statements below verbally.
2. Don't look at the tags given next to each statement.
3. Check to see if you are right.

You know it,	don't you?
Tom is handsome,	isn't he?
You can share your coffee with me,	can't you?
You wouldn't want to fight with her,	would you?

Learning Tips

- A great technique to avoid questioning errors is to remember that they begin with a question word (either wh-words, how, or helping verbs).

- To form sentences, we use, subject + verb + object. In questions, we place the verb before the subject.

- If you consciously avoid errors discussed in this chapter, you will start forming questions that grammatically correct.

- Do not speak incorrectly if you hear others speak incorrectly. Get into the habit of identifying errors.

- Make a note of questions you get confused with the **Personal Notes** section.

Questioning Tips

- Do not ask too many questions at the same time. It can bore or irritate the listener.

- After asking a question, give the other person time to respond.

- Keep your questions short and crisp. (Note: Apply this tip even while forming sentences. When you keep your questions and sentences short and crisp, you make lesser errors and are able to communicate better.

Personal Notes

____

____

____

____

Pronunciation Time

Why do people sound different? Some sound smooth and some sound robotic.

Sentence stress and intonation have a huge role to play in how a person sounds. You need to stress on words correctly and have a good intonation pattern if you want to sound good when you speak.

We will be covering sentence stress and intonation in the Pronunciation section.

Learning Tip: Before we begin Sentence Stress, practise saying:

- The consonant and vowel sounds aloud along with examples
- Common words by stressing on the right syllable

We stress *syllables* in a word to *pronounce words correctly*. Similarly, we stress *words* in a sentence to convey what we are saying correctly.

Let's take an example. Say the following sentence aloud while stressing the words in bold.

She **makes** the **best pasta.**

How do you know which words to stress?

There are two simple rules.

1. Stress the words that give out important information. These are called **content words.** We can also say that these are the **strong words** in a sentence.

2. Don't stress the words that don't give important information. These are called **function words.** They are used to join content words. We can also say that these are the **weak words** in a sentence.

Take a look at the table below to understand more.

Content Words	Function Words
Nouns: book, table	**Pronouns**: he, she, they, it
Main Verbs: make, cook	**Helping verbs**: is, am, are, could, may
Adjectives: good, bad, long, short	**Prepositions**: to, from, behind, on, over
Adverbs: loudly, angrily, joyfully	**Articles**: a, an, the
	Conjunctions: and, because, however

Content Words	Function Words
These words carry important information and are stressed.	These words don't carry important information and are not stressed. They are used to join content words.

Learning Tips

- When we say or read longer sentences, it gets difficult to break each word grammatically and then stress on it. Therefore, I recommend you understand the kind of words that give out important information through the table above. When you say or read sentences on a day to day basis, try to stress the important words and not to stress the words that join them.

- Do not stress on each word in a sentence. Doing this can make you sound like a robot.

- Stress the content words in a way so that the time between them is the same. Let's understand this through the example I gave earlier: She **makes** the **best pasta**.

  - In this sentence, the time between the following words when you say this sentence aloud should be the same:
    - *makes and best*
    - *best and pasta*
  - This means that the weak word, *the* has to be said quickly and without much stress.

- Make a conscious effort to speak with the right stress. Your sentence stress pattern would improve over a period of time.

- Read some English content loudly on a daily basis to practise.

Activity

Practise saying the following sentences aloud using the right stress. The important words that need to be stressed are given in bold.

These are sentences you reviewed while learning subject verb agreement. Reading these aloud will also help you remember the rules.

Harry does **magic.**
Harry and **Sunny do magic.**
The **boy**, who has **two laptops**, is a **genius.**
Girls, who own a **house**, are **lucky.**
Here are his **shoes.**
There is **no water** in the **glass.**
The **bride** and the **groom look happy.**
The **table** and the **chair** are **broken.**
Bread and **jam** is **tasty.**
Everything **confuses** me **these days.**
Most of the **people** are **educated.**
Most of the **population** is **educated.**
One of the **boys** is **laughing.**
Honey is **healthy.**
The **team** has a **good spirit.**
The **reality** is **painful.**
My **aunt** or **uncle** is **going** to **dance.**
Neither my **friend** nor his **cousins** are **fun loving.**
Either **you** or your **mother needs** to **cook.**
Either **Ronny** or his **sisters** have the **authority** to **sign** the **paper.**
Sheela, along with her **sons**, is **going** for the **movie.**
Noun as well as **verb** is **important.**
Emails as well as **phone calls** are **needed.**
Not only **fish** but also its **bones annoy** me.

Ten years is a **long time.**
Seven pounds is **too less** to **buy** that **item.**
Eight kilograms is **difficult** to **lose.**

Changing Stress

The rules above are good to identify which words to stress normally. However, the stress can change according to what you want to convey to the listener. The same sentence can have a different meaning based on the word you stress the most.

Say the following sentence in three different ways by stressing the word in bold.

- **I** love you. (means I love you, not John)
- I **love** you. (means I love you; not hate you)
- I love **you.** (means I love you; not her)

Learning Tip

Sentence stress is powerful. The meaning of what you say depends on how you stress the words in a sentence. Therefore, practise stressing the right words each time you speak in English.

Let us begin with **intonation.**

Say the following sentence aloud while stressing the words in bold.

She **makes** the **best pasta.**

While stressing on words, you automatically drop or raise your pitch at the end of words and especially when you complete a sentence. This creates intonation.

Intonation is the rise and fall of the voice while speaking. It is created by dropping or raising your pitch while speaking.

Without sentence stress and intonation, you would end up sounding robotic.

Intonation Patterns

There are various types of intonation patterns that are used when we say sentences, questions, numbers, and so on. We will review the most common ones. If you can use these correctly while speaking, you will be able to convey your message well.

Falling Intonation

- Drop your pitch.
- Use it while ending sentences and open-ended questions.

Rising Intonation

- Drop your pitch.
- Use it while ending closed-ended questions.

Falling and Rising Intonation

- Drop and raise your pitch.
- Use it in question tags.

Rising, Rising and Falling Intonation

- Raise, raise, and drop your pitch.
- Use it while giving options, reading lists, and numbers.

Falling Intonation

When you end sentences and open-ended questions, use falling intonation. In simple words, drop your pitch at the end of sentences and open-ended questions.

Take a look at the examples below and practise dropping your pitch at the end.

Harry does **magic.***(drop your pitch)*
Harry and **Sunny do magic.***(drop your pitch)*
The **boy**, who has **two laptops**, is a **genius.***(drop your pitch)*

What did she **write?** *(drop your pitch)*
What do they **think?** *(drop your pitch)*

Rising Intonation

When you end closed-ended questions, use rising intonation. In simple words, raise your pitch at the end of closed-ended questions.

Take a look at the examples below and practise raising your pitch at the end.

Do you **want water?** *(raise your pitch)*
Can you **eat fish?** *(raise your pitch)*
Can he **sing?** *(raise your pitch)*
Does he **like mangoes?** *(raise your pitch)*
Does she **speak well?** *(raise your pitch)*

Falling and Rising Intonation

- When you end the first part of the question tag, use falling intonation.
- When you end the second part of the question tag, use rising intonation.

Take a look at the examples below and practise dropping and raising your pitch.

You **know** it, *(drop your pitch)* **don't** you? *(raise your pitch)*
Tom is **handsome,** *(drop your pitch)* **isn't** he? *(raise your pitch)*
You can **share** your **coffee** with me, *(drop your pitch)* **can't** you? *(raise your pitch)*
You wouldn't **want** to **fight** with her, *(drop your pitch)* **would** you? *(raise your pitch)*

Note: The question words used in the tags are normally stressed.

Rising, Rising and Falling Intonation

When you give options to someone, use rising, rising and falling intonation. In simple words, raise your pitch at the end of each option and drop your pitch at the end of the final option.

Let's assume a guest has visited your house and you are giving options of what's there to drink.

- Raising your pitch at the end of *tea* and *coffee* tells the listener that there are more options.
- Dropping your pitch at the end of *water* tells the listener that there are no more options.

Would you like to **have tea,** *(raise your pitch)* **coffee,** *(raise your pitch)* or **water?** *(drop your pitch)*

Practise raising and dropping your pitch.

Please **give** me your **pen** *(raise your pitch)* and **pencil.** *(drop your pitch)*
The **number** is **1800** *(raise your pitch)* **222** *(raise your pitch)* **6666.** *(drop your pitch)*

Activity

Practise saying the following sentences and questions aloud using the right stress and intonation pattern. The more you practise, the better you will get at pronunciation.

- Drop your pitch at the end of sentences and open-ended questions.
- Raise your pitch at the end of sentences closed-ended questions.
- Drop your pitch when you end the first part of the question tag. Raise your pitch when you end the second part of the question tag.
- Raise and drop your pitch when there is more than one person or thing mentioned.

Sentences	Questions
Harry does magic.	What is your name?
Harry and Sunny do magic.	What do you like?
The boy, who has two laptops, is a genius.	What do you want to eat?
Girls, who own a house, are lucky.	Where do you live?
Here are his shoes.	What do you mean?
There is no water in the glass.	What is your name?
The bride and the groom look happy.	What do you like?
The table and the chair are broken.	What do you want to eat?
Bread and jam is tasty.	Where do you live?
Everything confuses me these days.	What are you doing?
Most of the people are educated.	Where are you going?
Most of the population is educated.	What are you staying?
One of the boys is laughing.	When does she leave the country?
Honey is healthy.	What does he want?
The team has a good spirit.	What did she write?
The reality is painful.	What do they think?
My aunt or uncle is going to dance.	What movie did you watch yesterday?
Neither my friend nor his cousins are fun loving.	What movie will you watch tomorrow?
Either you or your mother needs to cook.	When did he call?

Sentences	Questions
Either Ronny or his sisters have the authority to sign the paper.	What did she ask?
Sheela, along with her sons, is going for the movie.	Do you like cheese?
Noun as well as verb is important.	Do you want water?
Emails as well as phone calls are needed.	Can you eat fish?
Not only fish but also its bones annoy me.	Can he sing?
Ten years is a long time.	Does he like mangoes?
Seven pounds is too less to buy that item.	Does she speak well?
Eight kilograms is difficult to lose.	Did you watch a movie yesterday?
	Will you watch a movie tomorrow?
	Did he call?
	Did she ask him to practise?
	He is right, isn't he?
	He is not right, is he?
	She doesn't speak well, does she?

Learning Tip

To improve intonation and sentence stress,

- Listen to English speakers on T.V. and in real life.
- Think and speak in English.
- Read aloud passages written in English.
- Make a conscious effort to:

- - pronounce the consonant and vowel sounds correctly.
  - stress the right syllable.
  - stress the right word.
  - drop or raise your pitch correctly.
- Make a good speaker of English listen to you and give you feedback.

Self-Practice Activity

Watch another English movie or a programme on T.V. to get used to understanding English.

Now you can go back to the video game or wish list table given in Chapter 1 and tick Subject Verb Agreement, Question Formation, and Sentence Stress & Intonation.

Chapter 6

• • • • • • • • • •

ADJECTIVES, ADVERBS AND TONE

Remember, we mentioned adjectives and adverbs while learning sentence stress. These words are *stressed* while speaking as they give out important information.

We will cover this section by using a "Discovery" approach in which you will discover and use adjectives and adverbs through activities.

Let's begin!

Review the notes in the table below before beginning the discovery.

Adjectives	Adverbs
What are Adjectives?	**What are Adverbs?**
Words that describe or modify a noun or pronoun. In simple words, adjectives describe a person or thing.	Words that describe or modify a verb, adjective or another adverb. They answer questions like how, when, where, how much, how often about the word they are describing.

Adjectives	Adverbs
	Note: Adverbs modify phrases, clauses, and sentences too. We will not be getting into those details. If you have your basics right, you will get better as you practise speaking in English.
Examples: Rita is a *pretty* girl. (Describing a noun) I am *tall*.(Describing a pronoun)	**Examples:** Larry speaks *fast*.(Describing a verb) She is *very* nice. (Describing an adjective) They run *extremely* slowly. (Describing an adverb)
Comparative Forms These are used to compare two things. Usually formed by adding **–er** at the end of the adjective. Robert is *richer* than Bob. (Comparing two nouns) Your food is *sweeter* than hers. (Comparing two nouns)	**Comparative Forms** These are used to compare two words. Usually formed by adding **–er** at the end of the adverb. Emily types *faster* than Sheela. (Describing a verb) He works *harder* than his wife. (Describing a verb)
Superlative Forms These are used to compare three or more things. Usually formed by adding **–est** at the end of the adjective.	**Superlative Forms** These are used to compare three or more things. Usually formed by adding **–est** at the end of the adverb.

Adjectives	Adverbs
Your shoes are the *cleanest*. (Comparing nouns)	She slept the *longest*. (Describing a verb)
This rope is the *thinnest*. (Comparing nouns)	He answered the *quickest*. (Describing a verb)
Common Irregular Adjectives Their comparative and superlative forms are not made by from the rules above. Good, better, best Little, less, least Much, more, most Bad, worse, worst	**Common Irregular Adverbs** Their comparative and superlative forms are not made by from the rules above. Well, better, best Little, less, least Much, more, most Badly, worse, worst
Long Adjectives (Usually Four Syllables) For most longer adjectives, the comparative is made by adding the word **more**, for example, *more beautiful* and the superlative is made by adding the word **most**, for example, *most beautiful*. Reema is *more beautiful* than Simran. Reema is the *most beautiful* amongst the girls.	**Long Adverbs (Usually Four Syllables)** For most longer adverbs, the comparative is made by adding the word **more**, for example, *more beautifully* and the superlative is made by adding the word **most**, for example, *most beautifully*. Reema described the book in a *more beautiful* manner than Simran. Reema described the book in the *most beautiful* manner.

Activity

Information: Understanding Adjectives and Adverbs

From the table above, you know that:

- Adjectives describe a person or thing.
- Adverbs describe or modify a verb, adjective or another adverb.

Let's add a little more the definitions above.

- Adjectives can describe a person or thing in many ways such as their look, colour, shape, sound, quantity and so on.
- Similarly, adverbs can modify a verb, adjective or another adverb in many ways such as:
  - Describing the place where something happens
  - Describing the time or frequency at which something happens
  - Describing the manner in which something happens
  - Describing the degree to which something happens

Task

1. Take a look at the table below. It has types and examples of adjectives and adverbs along with sentences.
2. Think of one more example for each of type of adjective and adverb.
3. Form a sentence with the example you think of.

Adjectives	Adverbs
Appearance: gorgeous, cute	**Place:** here, there
Marsha is *gorgeous*. (How is Marsha to look at?)	Please go *there*. (Where do I go?)
Tony is *cute*. (How is Tony to look at?)	Keep the book *here*. (Where do I keep the book?)
Your Sentence:	**Your Sentence:**

Adjectives	Adverbs
Colour: black, yellow The book is *black*. (What is the colour of the book?) The shirt is *yellow*. (What is the colour of the shirt?) **Your Sentence:**	**Time:** sometimes, today He meets me *sometimes*. (How often does he meet?) I will dance *today*. (When will I dance?) **Your Sentence:**
Personality: kind, witty Marsha is *kind*. (How is Marsha as a person?) Tony is *witty*. (How is Tony as a person?) **Your Sentence:**	**Manner:** neatly, well She writes *neatly*. (How does she write?) He speaks *well*. (How does she speak?) **Your Sentence:**
Shape/Size: skinny, broad Marsha is *skinny*. (How is Marsha to look at?) Tony is *broad*. (How is Tony to look at?) **Your Sentence:**	**Degree:** little, greatly Sharon is a *little* generous. (How generous is Sharon?) He was *greatly* impacted by your comment. (How much was he impacted?) **Your Sentence:**
Sound: melodious, loud Marsha has a *melodious* voice. (How does Marsha sound?) Tony is *loud*. (How does Tony sound?) **Your Sentence:**	

Adjectives	Adverbs
Touch/Taste: hot, tasty Marsha eats *hot* food. (What kind of food does Marsha eat?) Tony's food is *tasty*. (How is Tony's food?) **Your Sentence:**	
Quantity: many, few Marsha has *many* dogs. (What is the number of dogs that Marsha has?) Tony has a *few* cats. (What is the number of cats that Tony has?) **Your Sentence:**	
Time: fast, quick Marsha is a *fast* runner. (How much time does Marsha take to run?) Tony is a *quick* learner. (How much time does Tony take to learn?) **Your Sentence:**	
Opinion: wonderful, best Marsha is *wonderful*. (What is your opinion of Marsha?) Tony is the *best*. (What is your opinion of Tony?) **Your Sentence:**	

Interesting Fact

Sometimes, the same word can be an adjective or adverb depending on how it is used in a sentence, for example:

- She writes the *best* books. (Adjective)
- She writes the *best*. (Adverb)

Activity

Information: Forming Adjectives and Adverbs

- We form adjectives from nouns, verbs, and even other adjectives. Here are a few examples:
  - Class (Noun) > Classy (Adjective)
  - Help (Verb) > Helpful (Adjective)
  - Blue (Adjective) > Bluish (Adjective)
- We form adverbs from adjectives. Here are a few examples:
  - Sad (Adjective) > Sadly (Adverb)
  - Sweet (Adjective) > Sweetly (Adverb)

Task

1. Take a look at rules for forming adverbs and adjectives in the table below.
2. Form adjectives and adverbs using the rules.
3. Check the answers to see if you are right.

Adjectives	Adverbs
Rules:	**Rules:**
There are many ways to change a word into an adjective. Here are some of them.	There are many ways to change an adjective into an adverb. Here are some of them.

Adjectives	Adverbs
<ul><li>Adding **-al** at the end of a word: magic>magical.</li><li>Adding **-y** at the end of a word: taste>tasty.</li><li>Adding **-ic** at the end of a word: academy>academic.</li><li>Adding **-ful** at the end of a word: beauty> beautiful.</li><li>Adding **-ous/-ious** at the end of a word: thunder>thunderous, glory>glorious.</li><li>Adding **-less** at the end of a word: shame>shameless.</li><li>Adding **-able/-ible** at the end of a word: depend> dependable, access>accessible.</li></ul>	<ul><li>Adding **-ly** at the end of most adjectives: beautiful > beautifully, magical > magically.</li></ul>

Note: These rules are given to help you form adjectives and adverbs. You will know which ending to use with different words when you practise communicating in English and listening to people who speak good English.

Not all adjectives and adverbs follow these rules, for example, good, bad, well, often, always and many more. These words can be adjectives or adverbs.

Adjectives	Adverbs
Change the following words into adjectives:	Change the following adjectives into adverbs:
• Economic >	• Excited >
• Understand >	• Rapid >
• Digest >	• Light >
• Breeze >	• Bland >
• Flake >	• Late >
• Allergy >	• Certain >
• Athlete >	• Proud >
• Harm >	• Horrible >
• Care >	• Logical >
• Fame >	• Mature >
• Melody >	• Amazing >

Answers

• Economic > Economical	• Excited > Excitedly
• Understand > Understandable	• Rapid > Rapidly
• Digest > Digestible	• Light > Lightly
• Breeze > Breezy	• Bland > Blandly
• Flake > Flaky	• Late > Lately
• Allergy > Allergic	• Certain > Certainly
• Athlete > Athletic	• Proud > Proudly
• Harm > Harmful/Harmless	• Horrible > Horribly
• Care > Careful/Careless	• Logical > Logically
• Fame > Famous	• Mature > Maturely
• Melody > Melodious	• Amazing > Amazingly

Activity

Do you remember the Syllable Stress rules we covered earlier? There were many long words we covered with endings such as -ic, -able, -ly and so on.

1. Review those rules and practise pronouncing the adjectives and adverbs we have used in this chapter.
2. Open an online dictionary to listen to the correct pronunciation.
3. Say each word aloud.

Activity

Information: Comparative and Superlative Forms

- Comparative forms are used to compare two things. Usually formed by adding **–er** at the end of the word.
- Superlative forms are used to compare three or more things. Usually formed by adding **–est** at the end of the word.
- For most longer words:
    - The comparative is made by adding the word **more** at the beginning
    - The superlative is made by adding the word **most** at the beginning.
- Irregular adverbs and adjectives are those whose comparative and superlative forms are not made by from the rules above.

Task

1. Create comparative and superlative forms of the adjectives and adverbs in the table.
2. Check the answers to see if you are right.

Adjectives	Adverbs
Regular: Short Words	**Regular: Short Words**
Example: Short, shorter, shortest Big: ______________, ________________ Old: ______________, ____________	Example: Fast, faster, fastest Hard:________________, ________________ Quick:________________, ______________
Regular: Long Words	**Regular: Long Words**
Example: Famous, more famous, most famous Gorgeous:______________, ____________ Harmful:______________, ____________	**Example:** Often, more often, most often Lightly: ________________, ______________ Intensely: ______________, ____________

Note:

- The comparative form of words that end with –y is made by removing the –y and adding ier.
- The superlative form of words that end with –y is made by removing the –y and adding iest.

Example: happy, happier, happiest

Irregular	Irregular
Examples:	**Examples**
Good, better, best	Well, better, best
Little, less, least	Little, less, least
Much, more, most	Much, more, most
Bad, worse, ajworst	Badly, worse, avorst
Many:______________, ____________	Far:______________, ____________

Answers

Adjectives	Adverbs
Regular: Short Words	**Regular: Short Words**
Example: Short, shorter, shortest	Example: Fast, faster, fastest
Big: bigger, biggest	Hard: harder, hardest
Old: older, oldest	Quick: quicker, quickest
Old: elder, eldest	
Regular: Long Words	**Regular: Long Words**
Example: Famous, more famous, most famous	**Example:** Often, more often, most often
Gorgeous: more gorgeous, most gorgeous	Lightly: more lightly, most lightly
Harmful: more harmful, most harmful	Intensely: more intensely, most intensely
Irregular	**Irregular**
Examples:	**Examples**
Good, better, best	Well, better, best
Little, less, least	Little, less, least
Much, more, most	Much, more, most
Bad, worse, worst	Badly, worse, worst
Many: more, most	Far: farther, farthest
	Far: further, furthest

Farther/Farthest Versus Further/Furthest

In the table above, we created two types of comparatives and superlatives for the word, **far**.

- When you are referring to distance that you can measure, use farther or farthest, for example:

- ◆ Sheena ran *farther* than I expected.
- ◆ Sheena ran the *farthest*.

- When you are referring to distance that you can measure, use further or furthest, for example:
  - ◆ I cannot delay *further*.
  - ◆ I have delayed to the *furthest*.

- When you are confused, use *further*. It's more acceptable.

The Word: Only

The word *only* can be an adjective or an adverb depending on which part of speech it is modifying in a sentence. A common confusion is: Where should it be placed in a sentence?

The answer is: It can be placed anywhere depending on what you want to convey. I should not be placed at the end.

- *Only* I speak in English. (Correct; means amongst everyone else, only **I** speak English.)
- I *only* speak in English. (Correct; means I only **speak** in English, not write in English.)
- I speak *only* in English.(Correct; means I speak only in **English**, not any other language.)
- I speak in English *only*. (Incorrect)

Listening Activity

Remember, you must develop a habit of recognising errors as you hear them and correcting them instantly. This activity will help you practise.

1. Read the following sentences loudly. They are wrong.
2. Try to identify the errors.
3. Correct each sentence verbally and check if you are right.

Wrong
Bob is more better than her.
She is the bestest.
She works more harder than Radha.
I am very much concerned about you.
I am from Delhi only.
I can go there even.

Right
Bob is better than her.
She is the best.
She works harder than Radha.
I am very concerned about you.
I am from Delhi only.
I can even go there.

Self-Practice Activity

Using adjectives and adverbs correctly requires practice.

1. Stand in front of a mirror and speak on each of the following topics in English for at least a minute.

    a. Describe someone you like or dislike

    b. Describe something you like or dislike

    c. Describe a sport

    d. Compare your room with your brother's or sister's room

    e. Luck or hardwork – what is better?

    f. Honesty is the best policy

2. Make a good speaker of English language listen to you when you speak.

3. Ask for feedback on Grammar and Pronunciation.

Note: If you don't have someone instantly available to listen to you, record your free speech and send your recording for evaluation.

Learning Tips

- Pick as many simple free speech topics as you can and speak on them for a minute. Do not start writing about them. The idea is to get conversational.
- Listen to native speakers of English on T.V. You will learn more adjectives and adverbs and also understand how they are placed in sentences.
- Do not speak incorrectly if you hear others speak incorrectly. Get into the habit of identifying errors.
- Make a note of anything new that you discover related to adjectives and adverbs in the section below.

Personal Notes

____

____

____

____

Pronunciation Time

Say the following sentence aloud in a happy way.

"I can speak in English."

Great! You just spoke in a *happy tone.*

Let's learn more about tone.

Learning Tip: Before we begin, practise saying:

- The consonant and vowel sounds aloud along with examples
- Common words by stressing on the right syllable
- The sentences given as examples or any passage in English with correct sentence stress and intonation

Say the following sentence aloud with the right sentence stress and intonation. But say it in a sad way.

"I am so happy today."

Does it sound funny? And were you able to express happiness?

This is the kind of impact tone can make to your message. You can have the best pronunciation, stress and intonation; however, you will not be able to convey your message properly if you don't use the right tone.

Tone has very little to do with what you say. It has a lot to do with *how you say it*.

What tone should you normally use while speaking?

This is how your tone should be when you speak on a day to day basis:

- Polite
- Friendly
- Energetic

If your tone has these elements, people would like to interact with you more. No one wants to speak to a person who always sounds dull.

Helpful Tips

To sound polite, friendly and energetic, there isn't much you need to do.

- Avoid speaking in a dull manner.
- Stay happy.
- Make a conscious effort to use a polite, friendly and energetic tone.
- Listen to motivational speakers who sound amazing. Notice that they sound like that because of using the right tone.

Remember: Using a polite, friendly and energetic tone will not only make you sound better but also attract more listeners.

Caution: Using an energetic tone does **not** mean that you start shouting. Very loud people are also not good speakers. You need to be audible but at the same time, do not bombard the listener with an overly loud voice.

Activity

1. Choose an English passage from a book or newspaper.
2. Practise reading it in a polite, friendly and energetic tone.
3. Remember to pronounce and stress the words correctly and use the right intonation pattern.
4. Make someone listen to you, if possible, and ask them for feedback on Tone and Pronunciation.

Self-Practice Activity

Watch another English movie or a programme on T.V. to get used to understanding English.

Now you can go back to the video game or wish list table given in Chapter 1 and tick Adjectives, Adverbs, and Tone.

Chapter 7

• • • • • • • • • •

PREPOSITIONS, ARTICLES AND FLUENCY

Imagine you are about to leave your house and you can't find your wallet. Suddenly someone tells you that it is *on* the table. And you smile!

This is the power of prepositions. They tell you where and when something is. In the above example, the preposition *on* tells you where the wallet is.

Let's begin with learning prepositions!

What are Prepositions?

Prepositions are words that are used with nouns and pronouns to show:

- Direction: The boy is *behind* you.
- Location: She is *at* his house.
- Time: I will complete the lesson *on* Thursday.
- Space: The pen is *under* the cupboard.

Can you make a sentence without prepositions?

Yes, for example, "Ram sang."

Note that this sentence is complete and grammatically correct; however, it does not give you much information.

If we say, "Ram sang *on her birthday*," the second part of the sentence gives more information.

In day to day language, we end up using prepositions a lot to give directions, to specify time, to explain where something is kept, to tell where someone is and a lot more.

Common Prepositions

There are many prepositions in English. Take a look at some of the most common ones.

> in, into, on, onto, at, since, for, from, behind, under, over, above, across, near, off, of, along, around, near, inside, beyond, between, down, up, till, until, by, before, beside, through, about

Preposition Usage

Prepositions are normally used with nouns, verbs, and adjectives. Sometimes, it gets hard to decide which preposition to use with a specific word.

Therefore, it's a good idea to know the common ones.

Nouns and Prepositions	Pronouns and Prepositions	Adjectives and Prepositions
After the noun: • A demand for • A need for • A reason for • An increase in • A decrease in • A fall in • A rise in • A relationship with/between	Prepositions are normally used after verbs. We also learnt earlier: (Verb + Preposition = Phrasal Verb) • Love to • Agree with/to	Prepositions are normally used after adjectives. • In love with • Similar to • Full of • Fond of • Short of/by • Interested in • Famous for

Nouns and Prepositions	Pronouns and Prepositions	Adjectives and Prepositions
• A connection with/between • A contact with/between • A solution to • A damage to • A key to • A reaction to • An answer to • A difference between • A plan of • A photograph of • A drawing of • The cause of	• Depend on • Pay for • Think about • Wait for • Rely on • Stuck to • Write to • Run away/to/into • Walk on • Make up • Look at/up • Talk to • Speak with • Cook for/from • Show up/from • Switch off	• Nice to • Good to • Bad to • Responsible for • Sorry for/about • Married to • Scared of • Upset about • Disappointed with • Satisfied about • Angry with/about/for • Proud of • Crowded with • Worried about
Before the noun: • For example • By chance • By mistake • By cheque • In love • On fire		

Nouns and Prepositions	Pronouns and Prepositions	Adjectives and Prepositions
• On the television • On the radio • On a trip • On a holiday • On a diet		

Interesting Fact: Did you notice that a variety of prepositions can be used with some words? Use them according to what you want to tell the listener.

Activity

1. Make a sentence verbally with each of the phrases given in the table above. Do not start writing as the idea is to discover the usage through a conversation.
2. Make someone who speaks English well listen to you and ask them for feedback.

Commonly Confused Prepositions

There are many prepositions. Rather than cramming the meaning of each of them, form a sentence whenever you get confused.

In/on/at

- *In* is the <u>least specific</u>.
- *On* is <u>more specific</u> than *in*.
- *At* is the <u>most specific</u>.

Example: I was born *in* December *on* 16 *at* 5 am.

To/for

Example: Give the book *to* her. It is *for* her.

For/since

- *For* is used when you can <u>measure time</u>.
  - Example: I have not met him for 2 years.
- *Since* is used when you <u>refer to a point of time</u>.
  - Example: I have not met him since 2005.

Under/underneath/beneath

Examples:

A: Put the leaf *under* her book.

B: Where should I put it?

A: *Underneath* the table.

B: Where exactly?

A: *Beneath* the black strip on the book.

Since/from

Examples:

I have been working *since* 7 am.

I work *from* 7 am to 5 pm.

To/from

Examples:

Give the bag *to* her.

Take the bag *from* her.

About/on

Examples:

She spoke *on* the topic, English.

She spoke *about* verbs.

Above and over

Examples:

Wear the sweater *over* your shirt.

Wear the pants *above* your waist.

Across and through

Examples:

Her house is *across* the road.

We need to go *through* the subway.

In/into

Examples:

The water is *in* the glass.

Pour the water *into* the glass.

On/Onto

Examples:

Keep the paper *on* the table.

Transfer the paper *onto* the table.

To/toward

Examples:

A: Come *to* the park.

B: How? I can only see a building.

A: Walk *toward* the building. The park is close *to* it.

Is it acceptable to end a sentence with a preposition?

Yes it is, till the time we are communicating verbally or in an informal manner. In formal writing, it is not acceptable to end a sentence with a preposition.

Examples:

Come *in*. (Informal)

Come *into* the room. (Formal)

Turn the fan *off*. (Informal)

Turn *off* the fan. (Formal)

Self-Practice Activity

Using prepositions correctly requires practice.

1. Stand in front of a mirror and speak on each of the following topics in English for at least a minute.

    a. Directions from the closest shopping centre to your house

    b. Your favourite recipe

    c. Locating your favourite outfit

2. Make a good speaker of English language listen to you when you speak.

3. Ask for feedback on Grammar and Pronunciation.

Note: If you don't have someone instantly available to listen to you, record your free speech and send your recording for evaluation.

Learning Tips

- Pick as many simple free speech topics as you can and speak on them for a minute. Do not start writing about them. The idea is to get conversational.

- Listen to native speakers of English on T.V. You will learn more prepositions and also understand how they are placed in sentences.

- Do not speak incorrectly if you hear others speak incorrectly. Get into the habit of identifying errors.

- Make a note of anything new that you discover related to prepositions in the section below.

Personal Notes

____

____

____

____

Articles

These are the articles in English.

a, an, the

Interesting Fact

An article is a kind of an adjective which gives some information about the noun, for example:

- I have *a* watch.

- I have *an* egg.

- This is *the* watch you gave me.

What is the difference between a, an, and the?

Definite Article		Indefinite Article
A	**an**	**the**
Used when a noun is non-specific or when we are talking in general. This article is similar to the number *one*, for example, "I have *a* watch" and "I have *one* watch" pretty much mean the same thing except that number *one* adds more emphasis.		Used when a noun is specific or when we are specifying something about the noun.

Used with nouns beginning with consonants.	Used with nouns beginning with vowels.	Used with nouns beginning with consonants and vowels.
I have *a* <u>watch</u>. I have *a* <u>brush</u>	I have *an* <u>egg</u>. I have *an* <u>umbrella</u>.	I have *the* <u>watch</u> you gave me. I have *the* <u>umbrella</u> he bought.

Common Errors

Most of the common errors with articles are made due to:

- Missing articles when they are needed.
- Adding the wrong article.

Therefore, we will review how to use articles with each type of noun.

Learning Tip: Focus on understanding the usage of articles with nouns through the rules.

Remember this table from the Nouns chapter?

Proper Nouns	Common Nouns
Ansh, Ruby, Sheru, India, Harry Potter, 3 Idiots, Sunday	boy, girl, elephant, dog, country, book, education, birthday

Let's review article usage with proper nouns.

- Do not use an article with proper nouns.
  - I went to *the America*. (Wrong)
 I went to *America*. (Right)

  - This is *the Bob Smith*. (Wrong)
 This is *Bob Smith*. (Right)

- Use *the* when the proper noun is collective or specific.
    - I went to *United States*. (Wrong)

      I went to *the United States*. (Right)

    - This is *Smith's residence*. (Wrong)

      This is *the Smiths' residence*. (Right)

Let's review article usage with the two major kinds of common noun – countable and uncountable.

Countable Nouns
photograph, book, key, phone, case, base

- Use *a/an* when the countable noun is singular and non-specific.
    - Click *photograph*. (Wrong)

      Click *a photograph*. (Right)

    - Give me *phone*. (Wrong)

      Give me *a phone*. (Right)

- Use *the* when the countable noun is specific, could be singular or plural.
    - *Photograph* he clicked was lovely. (Wrong)

      The photograph he clicked was lovely. (Right)

- Do not use an article if the countable noun is plural and non-specific. You could use the word *some*, if needed.
    - *Books* are helpful. (Right)

      Some books are helpful. (Right)

Uncountable Nouns
butter, cheese, honey, water, wood, rice

- Do not use an article if the uncountable noun is non-specific. You could use the word *some*, if needed.

- ◆ Please give me *water*. (Right)

  Please give me *some water*. (Right)

- Use *the* when the uncountable noun is specific.
  - ◆ *Water* in the green glass is dirty. (Wrong)

    The water in the green glass is dirty. (Right)

Interesting Fact

- Use *the* before mentioning a musical instrument in a specific way.
  - ◆ He has *a piano*. (Right)
  - ◆ He plays *the piano*. (Right)

Activity

1. Fill in the blanks with a, an, the. If there is no article needed, write no article.
2. Read the passage aloud while filling the blanks.
3. Check the answers to see if you are right.

_____________________Tony is_____________________nice boy. He collects_____________________pens. He gave me one of his pens._____________________green pen was_____________________best. Tony also drinks_____________________lot of_____________________ tea. Too much tea is harmful but_____________________tea that he drinks is herbal._____________________Herbal tea is healthy. I have asked Tony to get _____________________ few packets for me. He told me that it is only available in_____________________Assam. That's one of his favourite places. Tony eats_____________________egg everyday with_____________________milk._____________________milk that he drinks comes in special bottles. Tony is surely_____________________ lucky boy.

Answers

Tony is **a** nice boy. He collects pens. He gave me one of his pens. **The** green pen was **the** best. Tony also drinks **a** lot of tea. Too much tea is harmful but **the** tea that he drinks is herbal. Herbal tea is healthy. I have asked Tony to get **a** few packets for me. He told me that it is only available in Assam. That's one of his favourite places. Tony eats **an** egg everyday with milk. **The** milk that he drinks comes in special bottles. Tony is surely **a** lucky boy.

Listening Activity

Remember, you must develop a habit of recognising errors as you hear them and correcting them instantly.

1. Read the following sentences loudly. They are wrong.
2. Try to identify the errors. Correct each sentence verbally and check if you are right.

Wrong
He is good at speaking the English.
He is good at speaking English language.
The Bombay is a great place.
He plays guitar.
We live in city.
Do you want pen?
I have a news for you.
I have headache.
My mother is housewife.

Right
He is good at speaking English.
He is good at speaking the English language.
Bombay is a great place.
He plays the guitar.

Right
We live in the city.
Do you want a pen?
I have news for you.
I have a headache.
My mother is a housewife.

Self-Practice Activity

Using adjectives and adverbs correctly requires practice.

1. Stand in front of a mirror and speak on each of the following topics in English for at least a minute.

    a. House

    b. Job

    c. Butter

    d. The Himalayas

2. Make a good speaker of English language listen to you when you speak.

3. Ask for feedback on Grammar and Pronunciation.

Note: If you don't have someone instantly available to listen to you, record your free speech and send your recording for evaluation.

Learning Tips

- Think and speak in English to improve the usage of articles. It takes time and practise.

- Listen to native speakers of English on T.V.

- Do not speak incorrectly if you hear others speak incorrectly. Get into the habit of identifying errors.

- Make a note of anything new that you discover related to articles in the section below.

Personal Notes

Fluency Time

Have you ever caught yourself struggling to continue a conversation, blanking out while speaking or pausing a lot?

These are all issues related to fluency. Let's learn further.

Learning Tip: Before we begin, practise saying:

- The consonant and vowel sounds aloud along with examples
- Common words
- The sentences given as examples or any passage in English with correct sentence stress, intonation and tone.

Fluency is the ability to express yourself easily without breaking your thought flow. In other words, you will only be fluent if you are able to communicate smoothly in English.

Pronunciation, grammar, and comprehension – all of them impact fluency.

Barriers to Fluency and Improvement Techniques

Fluency can be a huge challenge for people who don't speak in English on a day to day basis. Here are some of the common factors due to which a person does not sound fluent. I have also listed techniques to overcome these barriers.

- **Unclear Thought Flow:** It means not knowing what to say next due to which you give out information in a confusing manner or stop talking. It happens when you don't mentally plan what you need to say. Even the best of speakers can face issues with fluency if they *don't mentally plan what they want to say.*

- **Techniques for Improvement**

  The mental planning that I am talking about doesn't need to take hours because you won't get that much time when you are communicating with someone. In writing, you may get an opportunity to plan or rewrite your message. Speaking doesn't work like that. The best way to speak fluently on any topic in the world is to answer three questions while you are explaining the topic. Given below are the three questions that I answer if someone asks me to speak on a topic.

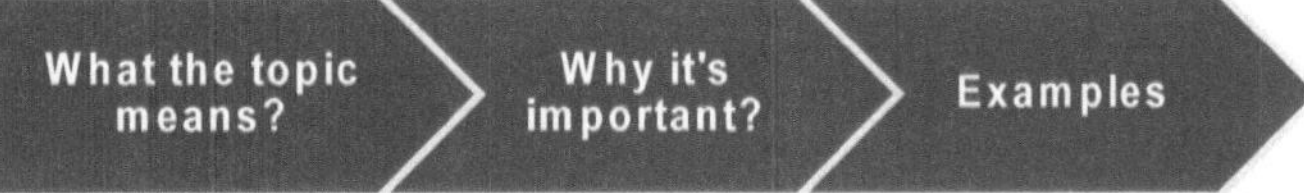

For example, if someone asks me to speak on the topic, **tea**, here is how I would explain it.

1. What is tea?

2. Why do people drink tea?

3. Examples of people I know of who drink a lot of tea or hate drinking it

Did you notice how I tried to organise the topic through the three questions. Let's say someone asks me to speak further, I would again answer another question.

4. What are the health benefits as well as health problems that can occur if a person drinks too much of tea?

If someone asks me to speak further, I would again answer more questions.

5. How does one make tea?

6. What are some tea brands?

Fluency is about being able to speak without another person constantly encouraging you or asking you questions to explain a topic. I am not saying that you need to always ask the questions that I mentioned above. The questions or their order could change depending on the conversation or context. What's important is to mentally ask yourself a few questions so that the information you give out is more organised. Be so fluent that even if you don't know anything about a particular topic, you can speak on the topic, "Why you don't know anything about that topic?"

Caution: Sometimes this technique makes people feel like you are talking or explaining too much especially if you are communicating with someone who is formal or doesn't talk a lot. In such cases, involve the person in the conversation by asking them if would like to hear further about the topic. I have had hilarious experiences where a few of my friends teased me on talking too much. I laugh with them and say, "at least I gave someone a reason to laugh."

Another important tip is to make shorter sentences. It's difficult for the other person to understand you when you give too much information in one sentence. It is also difficult to explain something easily when you make very long sentences.

- **Unconscious Translation from Mother Tongue to English:** It means thinking in your mother tongue and literally translating it into English. When you do this, you end up thinking of words to translate into English and it becomes difficult to find the right words. Even if you manage to find them, you might end up speaking grammatically incorrect

English as the word order of your translation may not match the word order used in the English language.

- **Techniques for Improvement**

  Thinking in English is the only way to overcome this challenge. If you think in English, you wouldn't need to translate anything. To think in English, you need to:

  - Read English books, newspapers, and content on the Internet.

  - Watch English movies, programmes, or even YouTube videos if you enjoy watching them.

  - Communicate with people who speak good English.

  - Speak in English for a minute on a variety of topics.

  - Write essays on a few simple topics if you find it extremely challenging to speak for more than a few seconds. However, after a few days, practise speaking on those topics verbally.

- **Broken speech/Pausing:** It means giving unnecessary pauses or pausing at the wrong time while speaking. This mostly happens because of incorrect word and sentence stress, bad intonation pattern or bad pronunciation. It could also happen because of unclear thought flow, not being able to form sentences or not knowing anything about the topic. The reasons could be many and are interlinked. Simply put, your speech is bound to be broken if you are not good with pronunciation and grammar.

- **Techniques for Improvement**

  Practise! Take responsible for improving your pronunciation and grammar by practising to speak in English as much as you can. Make a good speaker of the English language listen to you and give you feedback. Remember, pronunciation also includes sentence stress and intonation. Use right stress and intonation. Listen to speakers who have a good intonation and stress pattern.

- **Nervousness:** Nervousness in the context of fluency indicates that you don't sound fluent because of not having enough confidence to speak. It could be due to a number of reasons such as not knowing the topic, not being comfortable with the person you are communicating with, or not having a great day. It may also be that you feel embarrassed or scared to speak in English in the fear that you will speak incorrectly. This happens a lot when people go for a job interview that requires them to speak in English. I am telling you this from personal experience. Speaking confidently in such a situation is not easy unless you are very good with the language.

- **Techniques for Improvement**
  - Develop the right attitude. Give up your inferiority complex of not being able to speak in English correctly. Just because you can't speak in a language, it doesn't make you a bad or less talented human being. Try to learn the language for your advancement.
  - Don't be scared to speak in front of people who speak good English. If someone corrects you, take it as positive feedback for improvement. And, if someone makes fun of you, then you shouldn't even consider it as feedback. Ignoring them is the best policy.
  - Take a deep breath, plan your thoughts well and then begin to speak.

- **Fillers and Repetition:** This means using unnecessary words or repeating words while speaking to fill up the gap in conversation. It could be out of habit or nervousness. Fillers are words such as *uh, um, aa, like,* and *you know.* These are alright to use if they are used to fill up short gaps, dead air, or to acknowledge the other person. But they can totally make the listener lose interest in the conversation when used too many times. Repetition of words happens due to the same reasons and makes the conversation boring.

- **Techniques for Improvement**
  - ◆ Identify the fillers that you use and make a conscious effort to reduce them.
  - ◆ Record yourself while speaking on a topic. Listen to the recording and note the fillers, repetitive words and instances when you used them.
  - ◆ Identifying instances is important because that will tell you when you normally use fillers or repeat words. Once you know the pattern, you will be able to make a conscious effort to reduce them.

- **Incomplete information:** This means leaving sentences incomplete. It could be just a habit or due to disconnected thought flow.

Technique for Improvement

  - ◆ Try to recognise if you do this while speaking. If yes, make a conscious effort to reduce it.

- **Incorrect Rate of Speech:** Rate of speech is the rate at which you speak. Incorrect rate of speech is when you are speaking too fast or too slowly. People speak fast out of habit or they feel that the listener may not have the time to listen if they speak slower. If it's a habit, then it will take a conscious effort to correct. However, if it's a belief that the other person doesn't have the time to listen, then break out of it. People anyway won't understand you too well if you speak very fast. In addition, there is a possibility that you will miss out important information. Hence, it's better to speak at the right rate of speech. If they are in a hurry, they will tell you or get back to you. However, speaking fast unnecessarily will only make you sound silly and incomprehensible. The recommended average speech rate is between 120 to 150 words per minute. Try to adapt to this rate of speech while speaking. And, if you are one of those who speak too slowly either due to nervousness or habit or any other reason, you will need to increase your rate of speech to be a good speaker.

Techniques for Improvement

- Pick a free speech topic and speak on it for a minute or two. Record yourself when you do this.

- Send your recording to someone who can give you feedback on your rate of speech. If possible, send it to a native speaker of the English language as they will be able to identify if they can understand you at the rate at which you speak.

- Ask other people who are good at English to tell you if they are comfortable with understanding you when you speak at a certain rate.

- Once you have identified whether your rate of speech is fast or slow, correct it by reading English passages aloud, listening to native speakers of the language, and getting constant feedback.

- **Incorrect Volume of Speech:** Have you ever felt like closing your ears while listening to someone who is extremely loud? Or, have you got annoyed while listening to someone who speaks at a volume that is too low to understand. Avoid being that person whose volume of speech annoys people.

Technique for Improvement

- Ask people around you if they feel your volume of speech is good, too loud or too low. People who listen to you will be able to best judge whether their ears can tolerate your volume.

- If they can't, make a conscious effort to speak at the right volume.

Learning Tips

If you noticed, speaking fluently pretty much requires everything that you have been doing or learning till now:

- Pronunciation
- Grammar
- Practice activities – Reading, listening, speaking, identifying errors, thinking in English

Fluency gets better once you identify your challenge areas and make a conscious effort to correct them. You will notice a change in how you speak if you keep practising the recommended activities as much as you can.

- Do make a note of feedback that you get on fluency in the section below.
- Revisit and change the feedback once you start getting better.

Personal Notes

____

____

____

____

Self-Practice Activity

Watch another English movie or a programme on T.V. to get used to understanding English.

Now you can go back to the video game or wish list table given in Chapter 1 and tick Prepositions, Articles, and Fluency. Do not tick the self-paced activity section till you spend a month or two on practising them.

CONJUNCTIONS, INTERJECTIONS, CONDITIONALS AND COMPREHENSION

While learning the different parts of speech, did you wonder where you would categorise the following words?

like, and, because, but, as

These are all conjunctions. Let's learn more!

Conjunctions join words and phrases together. In other words, they connect two parts of a sentence.

Examples:

1. I want a pen *and* pencil.

2. I did not go there *because* it was very hot.

Notice the following difference in the examples above.

- The first example is connecting two independent parts that are similar.

I want a pen.	I want a pencil.	So we say: I want a pen *and* pencil.

- The second example is connecting one main part with a dependent part in the sentence.

I did not go there.	The reason was: it was very hot.	So we say: I did not go there *because* it was very hot.

When conjunctions join parts of a sentence that are grammatically equal or similar, they are called **coordinating conjunctions**.

When they join one main part with a dependent part in a sentence, they are called **subordinating conjunctions**.

Coordinating Conjunctions	Subordinating Conjunctions
and, but, or, nor, so, yet, for	if, because, before, since, once, till, until, whether, while, although, how, when, where, as
<ul><li>Rita *or* her sister likes singing.</li><li>Jamie is naughty *so* she teases everyone.</li><li>She knew I was unwell *yet* she arranged a party.</li></ul>	<ul><li>I will not go for the interview *as* John will be there.</li><li>I will sing *while* you play the guitar.</li><li>She will only listen *if* you speak politely.</li></ul>

Interesting Facts

- Question words such as *how, when* and *where* can be used as conjunctions when they connect two parts of a sentence or question, for example:
    - I have no idea *where* he has gone.
    - Can you tell me *how* this is done?
- Like nouns, conjunctions can be compound, for example:
    - As long as
    - Now that

- ◆ Provided that
- ◆ Even though
- Conjunctions can be used as a pair in a sentence.
  - ◆ Neither, nor
  - ◆ Either, or
  - ◆ Not only, but also

Self-Practice Activity

Activity – 1

1. Choose a passage in English.
2. Mark the conjunctions and observe how they are used.
3. Read the passage aloud and focus on understanding the usage of conjunctions.

Activity – 2

1. Listen to a native speaker of English language on T.V. or the Internet for at least five minutes.
2. Focus on conjunctions and their usage.

Activity – 3

1. Create a short story using the following information:
   - John likes to play the guitar.
   - Sarah likes to sing.
   - Bob enjoys listening to music.
   - John, Sarah and Bob are friends.
2. Share the story verbally with a good speaker of English language.
3. Ask for feedback on Grammar, Pronunciation and Fluency.

Now let's take a quick look at **interjections**.

Read the conversation aloud:

A: *"Hey!* I met him."

B: *Aha!* Did you ask him for his number?

A: *Oops!* I forgot.

All the words in italics and with an exclamation mark are interjections. They have no real grammatical value but you may use them to make the conversation more interesting.

Notice that sentences can be complete without interjections. They simply make the conversation more expressive. They are not used in writing unless you are writing a conversational story.

Let's look at some more interjections.

> **ouch, yum, nah, dear, alas, hi, hello, well, uh**

Caution: Avoid using interjections as fillers.

Now let's take a quick look at **conditionals**.

There are times we use conditions in our sentences, for example, "if I had hundred shoes, I would…". When we use complex sentences like these, it becomes difficult to understand which tense to use. These four simple rules will help you form conditions in an easy way. I personally find them very helpful.

The Zero Conditional	If + simple present…use simple present tense	If you <u>melt butter</u>, it <u>turns</u> into liquid.
The First Conditional	If + simple present…use simple future tense	If you <u>go</u> there, you <u>will</u> <u>understand</u> how she is.
The Second Conditional	If + simple past…use would + base form of the verb	If I <u>took</u> the decision, I <u>would</u> <u>listen.</u>
The Third Conditional	If + past perfect…use would have + verb used in the past perfect tense	If I <u>had taken</u> the decision, <u>I would</u> <u>have listened.</u>

- Use the zero conditional while stating a fact or generic truth.
- Use the first conditional during conversation in general.
- Use the second and third conditional during conversation about the past.

Activity

While conditionals help us speak grammatically correct English, they can get confusing if not understood properly. Therefore, let's practise a little.

1. Fill in the blanks with the right verb form and tense.
2. Check the answers to see if you are right.

- If you eat too much, you _______ (puke).
- If you don't like her, _______ (tell) her to leave.
- If you had known her decision, you _______ (meet) her.
- If you spoke to the child, you _______ (be) more polite.
- If I make tea, you _______ never _______ (drink) it.
- If I had a wand, I _______ (do) magic.
- If I had danced, we _______ (win).

Answers

- If you <u>eat</u> too much, you <u>will puke</u>.
- If you don't <u>like</u> her, <u>tell</u> her to leave.
- If you <u>had known</u> her decision, you <u>would have met</u> her.
- If you <u>spoke</u> to the child, you <u>would be</u> more polite.
- If I <u>make</u> tea, you <u>will</u> never <u>drink</u> it.
- If I <u>had</u> a wand, I <u>would do</u> magic.
- If I <u>had danced</u>, we <u>would have won</u>.

Self-Practice Activity

1. Complete the story:
   - If I had fifty books, …
   - If you give me ten days, …
   - If you hire me for the job, …
   - If I had met her, …
   - If I could fly, …
   - If I knew, …
2. Speak for at least a minute or two.
3. Share the story verbally with a good speaker of English language.
4. Ask for feedback on Grammar, Pronunciation and Fluency.

Comprehension Time

Did you notice that I have been asking you to watch English movies and programmes since the beginning?

A simple reason for this is to improve comprehension.

Comprehension is the ability to understand something. In our case, we are specifically going to learn tips for understanding English.

Improvement Tips

- Watch English movies, programmes, and online videos that interest you.
- Use English captions as subtitles.
- Interact with people who speak good English.
- Notice the stress pattern they use, how they pronounce certain words, and how they connect certain words that make them sound fluent.

- Use an online dictionary and listen to the pronunciation of simple words you hear in a daily basis:
  - Days, weeks, and months in a year
  - Numbers

Remember, don't just hear English, listen to it by focusing on the sounds, stress pattern and speech pattern.

Chapter 9

• • • • • • • • • •

SUM IT UP

By now you must have ticked all of the topics in the Video Game or the Wish List table. I suggest not to tick the self-paced activities unless you practise them for a month or two. That's when you will notice a difference.

Here are some basic reminders and tips to improve in each of these areas throughout your life:

Grammar

- Make short and crisp sentences.
- Use singular and plural correctly.
- Use the correct tense.
- Practise free speech as much as you can.
- Interact with good speakers of the English language.

Pronunciation

- Practise and pronounce the consonant and vowel sounds correctly.
- Stress the right syllable in a word.
- Stress the right word in a sentence.
- Practise speaking in a polite, friendly and energetic tone.

Fluency

- Organise thoughts or information before sharing them.
- Speak at the right rate of speech.
- Use the right tone and volume.
- Avoid fillers, repetitions and gaps.
- Complete your sentences.
- Take a deep breath if you get nervous.

Comprehension

- Listen, listen, and listen to native speakers of English in movies, programmes, or on the Internet.

Hope you enjoyed learning the language! It's time for you to take responsibility to practise. That's what I did and still do when I get stuck with anything.

Remember to stay motivated and not feel inferior as not knowing a language does not make you a bad human being.